THE
BIG BLACK
RUGBY
BOOK

Published by

rugby press ltd

Auckland, New Zealand.

©1990 Rugby Press Ltd
First published in 1990
Rugby Press Ltd
PO Box 100-243, North Shore Mail Centre, Auckland 10

ISBN 0-908630-33-6

Cover design : Michael Codling
Book design : Aidan Bennett, Helene Anderson
Typeset by Harlen Graphics, Glenfield, Auckland
Printed by Rodney & Waitemata Times, Warkworth

COVER PHOTOS: *John Kirwan, Craig Innes and
Zinzan Brooke in action during the triumphant
All Black tour of Wales and Ireland in 1989.*
Photo by : KENJI ITO

CONTENTS

DEDICATION

To the rugby players of tomorrow.

INTRODUCTION

By ZINZAN BROOKE

It gives me great pleasure to introduce *The Big Black Rugby Book*, which has the support of the 1990 All Blacks. Initially the plan was to call it *The Book for Boys*, for it is aimed specifically at the younger reader, but then we thought a name like that might stop Mums and Dads and girls buying it. Which would be a shame, because there's plenty in it for them too.

As All Blacks we seek to be innovative, to entertain, to reflect all that's good in rugby.

And hopefully you'll discover those same qualities in *The Big Black Rugby Book*.

The book is something quite delightfully different. Like the best rugby teams it sets out to entertain.

I'm sure that by the time you've read through The Making of The Good, The Bad and The Rugby and the Doc and Abo chapters you'll be closer to understanding what it's like touring overseas with an international rugby team. The training and the matches are tough, but we balance that with our own entertainment and camaraderie away from the playing field.

There's a nice blend of the old and the new in the book.

You can re-live some of New Zealand rugby's greatest games of the past 15 years and recall the highlights of the first World Cup while pondering the draw for the 1991 event in the UK and calculating which teams will advance to the grand final at Twickenham.

The 100 question quiz prepared by *Mastermind* finalist Grant Harding will let you know how you rate as a rugby authority.

Perhaps you should save the quiz till last, because you'll certainly know a considerably lot more about rugby after you've finished *The Big Black Rugby Book*.

The All Blacks have enjoyed their input into the book. We hope you derive as much satisfaction from reading it.

Good reading.

THE MAKING OF THE GOOD, THE BAD AND THE RUGBY

By RIC SALIZZO

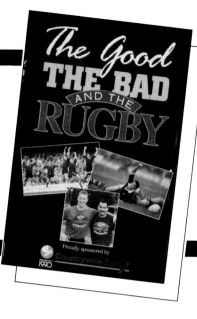

"The Good The Bad and The Rugby", the name came in a weary state in a hotel room in Cork, Ireland about three o'clock in the morning.

Stuck inside my head was that tune from a certain western thanks to All Black prop Ron Williams demonstrating his whistling skills. (He's very good.)

The Good, The Bad and The Ugly, not a bad movie DaDaDaDaa Daa Daa Daa. Not a bad description of a rugby tour.

What about The Good, The Bad and The Rugby, the man's a genius (although at three o'clock in the morning in a Cork hotel room, we all think we are pretty clever).

So after checking with my fellow producer, JJ Kirwan, we had a name for the video. Now all we had to get was a video.

It was a project that was carefully planned . . . okay, I'm telling lies.

It was a project hastily thrown together at the last minute.

In fact, when we left New Zealand, no one really knew what the end product would be.

With the approval of the team, our basic operations plan was: "If it moves, film it; if it doesn't move, kick it, then film it."

So, from day one we started filming. We filmed the players picking up their kit, we filmed them putting down their kit. We filmed them taking their gear into their rooms, we filmed them walking out of their rooms. We filmed them getting ready for their photo, we filmed someone else filming someone else taking their photo.

It was about that stage that it was suggested to the director: "Perhaps we should be a bit more selective." Point taken.

To start with, the film crew and I split up. They headed off to London with tape editor Bill Denton while I flew to Canada with the team for the first game.

Thanks to Air New Zealand I flew first class (which was most appreciated, can I do it again?).

However, the gloss of travelling in luxury was soon spoilt by a large man next to me, a certain Mr K Quinn. Stretched out, he seemed determined to match the noise of the jet engines with his snoring. He certainly was doing pretty well, good enough to drive me back to economy.

On travelling back to the rear of the plane I was accosted by two smilers, one an English gentleman by the name of Mr J Gallagher, the other a moustachioed Samoan, a Mr J Schuster.

"What's the movie on up there in first class?"

"Don't know," was the educated reply.

"Want us to go up and check for you?"

"Thanks guys, that's really good of you."

That was the end of my first class status.

Because the film crew was in London, filming in Canada was kept to a minimum because we had to use a freelance camera crew at a cost of about $2000 per day.

JK and I decided one thing we would have to film was the boys at a Canadian football game. The night of the game I had to do some work (yes, Mr Stanley, I know that's unusual) but I arranged to meet the team at the stadium.

That sounded good in theory but, in practise, finding 30 blokes in a massive double decker dome which seats 60,000 is not too easy.

By halftime, with still no sight of the All Blacks, we were about to give up the search but we were saved by the public address system.

"Ladies and gentlemen," it said in a Canadian accent, "tonight in the stadium we are privileged to host the world champion rugby team, the All Blacks. They're up there in block H, so give them a hand."

Of course, by this stage, most of the team had got bored and returned to the hotel so the ovation was greatly appreciated by those remaining who have now given the Canadians the impression that rugby is a game played by teams of five.

Canada was too much fun, so we had to leave and head to Wales where the people weren't so happy.

The first bit of filming was to be the opening press conference at a hotel near Heathrow.

It was shaping up to be quite a nasty affair with the British Press doing their best to stir up controversy over Buck Shelford's amateur status.

Everyone was on edge, the All Black management because they didn't want the tour to start on the wrong foot and Fleet Street because this was their chance to nail the unsmiling giants.

However, as it turned out, there were plenty of smiles all around as the All Blacks and their hosts spoke of how much they were looking forward to the tour and when the question of professionalism was brought up there was a polite no comment and that was it.

So much for the fiery Fleet Street press.

First stop was Cardiff where we were told we couldn't do any filming on the sideline during any matches on tour.

That was a fairly major problem as sideline action constituted half of our plans and it seemed no amount of pleading, shouting, crying and throwing temper tantrums was going to allow us to get our way.

However, a few quiet words from All

ALAN WHETTON and Sean Fitzpatrick check out a valuable sire during a visit to stud near Dublin.
Photo by : PETER BUSH

Black manager John Sturgeon and suddenly everyone was very helpful.

The first test of JK's skills as an interviewer was Matthew Ridge on the eve of his first match for the All Blacks.

Matthew turned out to be great interview talent; in fact, once he was switched on he was difficult to switch off. So pleased were we with that first interview that perhaps one day we might even make a whole documentary about Ridge.

The Cardiff game went without a hitch. The All Blacks won, we did our filming and it was onwards and upwards.

During the build-up for the next game Mr Kirwan found his achilles was hurting a little and he suggested we get some shots of Abo the All Black sadist inflicting some pain, sorry treatment.

However, luck was not to be on my fellow video producer's side. The match against Pontypool started in fine form. There were tries galore as the backline snapped into action. And then JK's achilles snapped into inaction.

On the sideline we weren't 100 per cent sure what was wrong so after the game the crew and I started to look for our star.

"Hey, Sleazo, I have a message for you," said Mr Fox, "JK said he'll meet the film crew at the Royal Gwent Hospital. He's snapped his achilles and he thinks it will be a good idea to get some shots of the operation."

Now that was a good news, bad news situation. The bad news was that John Kirwan was to become a permanent member of the injured tiki tours group. The good news was that even in times of extreme adversity he was thinking about getting the right pictures. Obviously he was learning the craft well.

Because I had to feed a story back to New Zealand, Mr K Quinn was despatched with the crew to the hospital, where a drugged-up JK turned in an inspired injured person performance. Co-starring was the doctor John Mayhew, dressed in funny clothes,and the concerned physio David Abercrombie.

And as he was being wheeled into the operating theatre Mr Kirwan would be heard arguing with the surgeon about the possibility of the crew being allowed into the operating theatre.

Fortunately they weren't allowed.

Once the co-producer had hobbled back to the team, he was advised to stay in Britain for medical reasons. That was good because I had plenty of work for him to do.

There weren't too many highlights in the next few games. The All Black injury toll kept mounting. So did the attacks on the referees.

The crowd kept pointing out how lucky the All Blacks were because they kept beating the Welsh teams. I almost got into several punch-ups with members of the crowd whose level of abuse shocked a young man like myself from a reputable Catholic school but fortunately my Italian temper was kept in check.

Newport came like a breath of fresh air.

The All Blacks played tremendous football and for the first time in ages we were able to work in the sunshine. Things were looking up.

The build-up for the test was a definite highlight.

Lunch was at a little country pub which showed off the best side of Wales and although competing with Spielberg Productions we were able to get some interesting footage, though we were scooped on the Botica, Schuler ice cream eating competition.

We thought the setting was ideal to interview the new test caps but as we tried to sneak Bachop and Innes aside we were followed by a gaggle of All Blacks. Less than impressed with my interviewing talents it was suggested I should relax for a while so they could take over.

However, it took only one interview

attempt from Matthew Ridge before I was called back into action.

As Graeme Bachop started to reveal his innermost thoughts we noticed that the would-be interviewers had now switched their attention to some very small horses.

Zinzan Brooke, the Northland farm boy, was preparing to give a demonstration of his riding talents. Zin was about three times as big as his chosen mount, prompting the call from coach Wyllie: "Zinny, get off that horse — you'll break it!"

All lighthearted fun until Richard Loe let the horse go and man and beast were out of control. They say a picture is worth a thousand words; Zinzan Brooke's face was certainly worth a video.

Of course we were now at the serious part of the tour, Test Day.

The Welsh were giving themselves a bit of a chance in this one and so they were in a fairly good mood. It seemed we had only to poke the camera and microphone into a pub and instant chorus' proclaiming the mighty Welsh rugby team burst forth.

We also pointed the camera at a Maori bloke in the street and he burst into a haka.

The Welsh would have sung along but they didn't know the words.

There wasn't too much singing done after the match by the Welsh; in fact, one bloke, a certain Mr John Dawes, seemed quite annoyed by the day.

He was in charge of press access under the grandstand. At first he wouldn't let us and Peter Bush in until Mr Wyllie quietly persuaded otherwise.

Dawes wasn't being selective. He let the

THE All Blacks entertaining as they train in Cardiff during their 1989 tour. Alex Wyllie's team were far ahead of the Welsh and the Irish in training methods.

Photo by : PETER BUSH

BBC crew down to do their post match interviews but he wouldn't let the interviewer down because they already had enough people.

The crew and I were shepherded into a room and told to stay there. Staying there meant we weren't allowed to take one step across the threshold, meaning we had to do a lot of yelling.

Fortunately the mountain came to Mohammed and Benny was able to interview his team mates while I looked after the tripod (a new found vocation).

It was then off to Ireland minus our film editor who together with his gear was too heavy for the plane.

Ireland is not Wales and therefore everyone was happy. Enough said.

We had the usual arguments about where we were able to film from but most people were pretty helpful.

A definite highlight was stopping off at the Young Munster club in Limerick, of which Z Brooke and R Williams are honorable members.

It was due to be a short stop off but the mood dictated otherwise and several very enjoyable hours were spent singing and laughing in the company of the Young Munsters.

For me it is a particular highlight of the video which is surprising considering some of the footage is shot by Graeme Bachop after he quietly borrowed the TV camera from Peter Day. Sound man Wayne Johnson did his bit by singing along.

After drinking a little orange juice a few stops along the trail were essential. As usual, our little mini van followed behind the All Blacks bus which was driven by a crazy man.

Eventually we hit Dublin again, the town of the mighty Ronnie Cosgrove and Derek the Yeeha specialist.

Again we were told we couldn't do any filming at the test match but we got around that by getting two seats in the front row and filmed from there.

Because there was no room for me

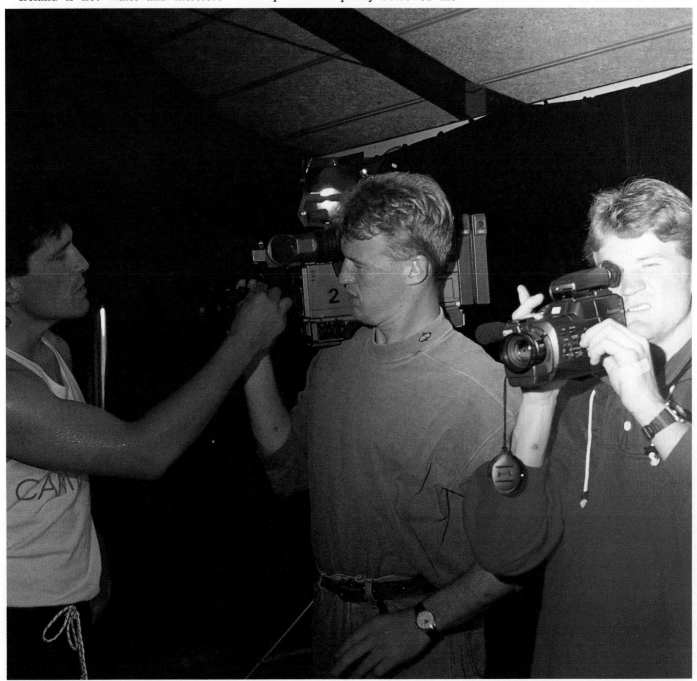

SPIELBERG PRODUCTIONS team — Zinzan Brooke, John Kirwan and Bernie McCahill — readying for a "shoot" during the tour of Wales and Ireland.   Photo by : PETER BUSH

JOHN GALLAGHER, named international player of the year after his performances on the UK tour, pressures Wales at the National Stadium in Cardiff.

Photo by : RUSSELL CHEYNE, Allsport

I headed off to the commentary box to examine the arts of Messrs Quinn, Nisbett and Kirton.

Of course I didn't have the right pass to be there so one chap made it his private mission to throw me out. Eventually I just leaned on the door so he couldn't come in and he gave up.

After a tremendous match JK decided it would be a good idea to talk to the front row. They suggested doing the interview in the shower but again an official stood in the way. He was very helpful and features in the end credits of the video.

Next stop was Northern Ireland which turned out to be a nice place but we had certain rules. When JK or I wanted something filmed we weren't allowed to call out to the cameraman to shoot; a dangerous choice of words.

By the time we hit London we had another battle on our hands to film at the game. Because the match is already filmed for television by an outside broadcast unit some rugby officials didn't see the need for another camera.

In fact what we were trying to do was offer another perspective with close-up shots from the sideline which often look more dramatic.

Twickenham of course isn't too keen on words such as "new perspective" but we circumnavigated that problem by getting six seats — three in the front row at one end and three in the front row at the other.

The sense of relief after that game was enormous, no more arguments. Sorry, just one more.

Trying to get some shots under the stand, a very determined man did his best to get in our way. Despite the team having no objections to our filming, he did.

Every time the camera was switched on he would jump up and down in front of it. For his efforts he, too, gets an appearance on the video and credits.

People like that were the exception. Most realised that what we were trying to do was beneficial to the game. We were showing one of the best teams of all time on tour.

We were trying to show that the All Blacks were in fact nice guys and not the unsmiling giants some had presented them as. There are seldom many better advertisements for the game than its players on a tour that has its good, its bad and its rugby.

Of course, next up is France where The Good, The Bad and The Rugby will continue.

The 1990 All Blacks to France, "Black et Bleu". ■

THE All Black squad for the Welsh test take a break from training in Cardiff. Hooker Sean Fitzpatrick holds the ball while skipper Wayne Shelford adopts his regular No 8's position.   Photo by : PETER BUSH

Ric Salizzo is a sports journalist with Television New Zealand.
A former senior rugby player he has specialised in rugby presentations. He won the 1990 New Zealand television journalist's award for his outstanding production *The Good, The Bad and The Rugby*.

MICHAEL JONES
– HAVING THE FAITH TO MAKE IT BACK

By HEATHER KIDD

Rugby posts in the backyard feature in Michael Jones' earliest recollections of the sport. He was just four years old when his father erected the poles and Jones remembers happy hours spent outdoors with his dad and elder brother, hours spent passing the ball and having fun.

Sadly that recollection is one of few he has of his father who died before Jones' fifth birthday.

But the love of rugby was never lost. His father, like so many Kiwis, was an avid rugby fan and Jones' mother, although Samoan, had also been brought up in a family where rugby was a popular pastime.

But rugby was not the only sport enjoyed by the Jones family and although Michael first played the game as a seven-year-old for the Te Atatu club he also found the time to play league.

He alternated between the two sports until he turned 10 and then, largely because of his school's influence, he began to focus on rugby.

By his own admission Jones was a little slower than many of his peers to develop mentally. Physically he was always quite big for his age and after muddling his way through the lower grades, by first XV level he realised he could mix it with the older kids and began, he says, to play good rugby.

Although he has captured world attention as an openside flanker Jones spent his early rugby years playing in the backs, mostly at second-five and centre.

He represented Roller Mills as an inside centre but his time in the backs came to an abrupt halt following a nasty accident with barbed wire, suffered during his third form year.

After a month in plaster he began to take his first tentative steps and he was dismayed to find he had lost a lot of speed. Still young he didn't realise it would take time for the injury to heal properly and decided his lack of pace was permanent.

He discussed the problem with his brother who advised him to move into the forwards where speed would not be as crucial. No one knew it then but an All Black of the future was on his way.

Even then Jones did not go straight on to the flank. His years in the first XV at Henderson High were spent as a No 8 and it wasn't until John Hart selected him for Auckland that he played on the openside.

During 1986 he played at No 8 for Auckland and the following season, World Cup year, he took over as the All Black openside flanker.

Jones was, without a doubt, the individual star of the World Cup tournament. The All Black team reached a standard of performance seldom witnessed in the rugby world and Jones was the shining light.

Captain David Kirk may have been the glamour boy off the field but Jones' wonderfully athletic displays on the paddock exemplified everything that was good about the game.

To Jones rugby is just that — a game. He is grateful for the natural talents he possesses which have helped him achieve success in the sport but he keeps his feet firmly on the ground because, for him, his love of God is the most important factor in his life.

His faith, he says, helps him keep everything in perspective. Rugby certainly plays a big part in his life but it is by no means everything.

Jones explains: "My faith gives me my motivation. I am very proud to represent my province and my country in sport and happy to use the talents that were given me but I use them, not for my own glory, for the glory of God.

"Rugby has proved an amazing medium to put across my point of view. New Zealanders are so sports minded and especially keen on their rugby. I've made my stand on certain matters but it's not just about being a christian. There are normal responsibilities that go with being an All Black and for me those have been easier to cope with because of my faith.

"It has meant I am able to accept things, such as the injury last year, and I have the strength to carry on.

"The impact of my injury was lessened because of my faith. I didn't find it hard to come to grips with."

Jones' rugby year came to an abrupt and painful halt in 1989 during the second test against the Argentinian Pumas played in Wellington. Jones went down heavily in a tackle and his knee collapsed.

He was carried from the field and after the doctor's examination flown straight back to Auckland for surgery. The damage was serious and many doubted Jones would ever play again but slowly, determinedly, he has made his way back to full fitness.

Jones would love to again pull on the All Black jersey. It is, he says, an awesome experience going out on the field to play for one's country.

Rugby has given him much — an appreciation of the passion the game engenders throughout New Zealand but especially in the smaller provinces and a realisation that so many Kiwis hold the game and the All Blacks in awe.

Because of rugby Jones has travelled overseas and experienced different cul-

MICHAEL JONES . . . back in action for Auckland during its Ranfurly Shield campaign in 1990.

Photo by : KENJI ITO

tures, something he is more than just mildly interested in.

Following a seventh form year at Henderson High, he went to Auckland University and gained a Bachelor of Arts. He followed this with a degree in town planning and is currently in his last year of an MA, majoring in geography.

The study of people and their environment has always interested Jones. His father was a geography teacher and he imagines his love of the subject stems from his parent.

His thesis is based on the effects of tourism in Western Samoa, looking at the impact the development of that industry would have on the island's environment at different levels — economic, social and political.

To research his paper Jones spent the summer months in Western Samoa and got much more than he bargained for. Cyclone Ofa struck while he was there and the excitement of being caught up in a real storm soon turned to anxiety as the tempest raged unabated.

Although damage to housing and crops was severe the human cost was not as high as first feared. Jones, along with his relatives, spent weeks involved in the mop-up operation and it was some time before he was able to resume both his studies and fitness programmes.

His delayed return to New Zealand prompted suggestions from some quarters that Jones lacked the drive to return to the top. Jones disagrees.

"I'm just like any other Kiwi rugby player and I want to be an All Black. I'm out of the team now but it's a real challenge for me to try and make it back."

He's on his way. His knee stood up to the rigours of a couple of club games but his comeback was hampered by a hamstring injury. Now fully recovered he returned to the rugby paddock in August to play his first rep game of the season for the Auckland C team.

He was then included in the Auckland B line-up and by early September he was back in the Auckland A side as it counted down to the serious end of the season and its defences of the Ranfurly Shield and national championship title.

Hard work and discipline have helped Jones make it back. "I knew it wasn't going to be easy," he admitted. "It's not just a matter of waking up one day and finding, hey presto, I'm back in the rep side.

"I've had to work hard to make it back this far. I've had to listen and learn from those trying to help me, it's the same as for anything else in life. Nothing just happens, you've got to make the most of opportunities that come along."

One of the biggest factors in Jones' struggle back to fitness has been his love of the game of rugby.

"That, for me, is the bottom line. I play because I enjoy the game. The day I don't enjoy it any more I'll stop playing."

New Zealand rugby fans will hope that day is a long way off. ■

THE controversial "no-scrums" shield challenge versus Canterbury, 1990. Here Michael Jones shapes up against Canterbury's Dallas Seymour.

Photo by : KENJI ITO

Heather Kidd as the assistant editor of *Rugby News* became the first woman to be attached to major international touring teams. A novelist and successful journalist she was named New Zealand sports writer of the year for 1990. She currently lives in Limerick, Ireland, where her husband is rugby coaching.

DOC AND ABO
– THE BACKROOM BOYS

By DEAN McLACHLAN

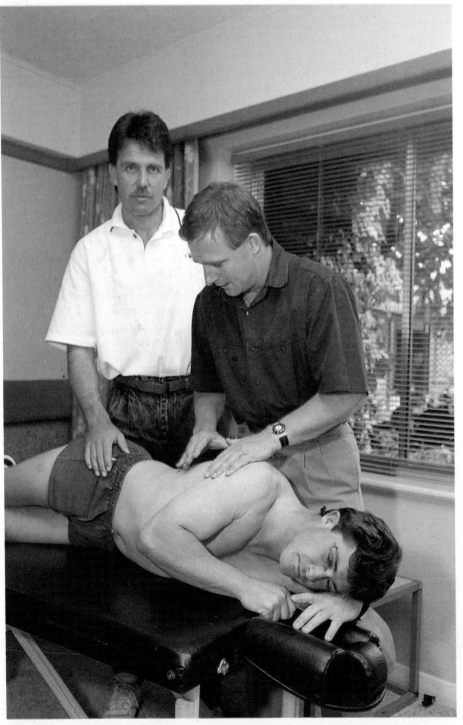

NEW All Black Paul McGahan is checked out by Doc (Dr John Mayhew, left) and Abo (physiotherapist David Abercrombie) before the team's departure for France in October.   Photo by : PETER BUSH

"They're very much part of the team. If they weren't so good at their jobs you'd forget they were the doctor and physio!"

The speaker is All Black superboot Grant Fox. The subjects are team doctor John Mayhew and physiotherapist Dave Abercrombie.

Abercrombie's been rubbing the players up the right way since the All Black tour to Japan in late 1987.

Dr Mayhew's been just what the team ordered since the tour of Australia the following year.

Both have played senior rugby. They're so familiar with the game they take part in team trainings.

Both are only in their mid-30s. So they're of an age to relate to all the players.

But, above all, both are well qualified. They've made such a mark the NZRFU has appointed them in principle through to the end of next year, inclusive of the World Cup.

John Mayhew graduated from Auckland University with his medical degree 13 years ago and four years later undertook a post-graduate course in sports medicine in London.

He runs a general practice in Birkenhead on the North Shore which has a heavy sports medicine bias. He also has a share in a sports medicine clinic in Auckland with Dr Tony Edwards.

At 1.90m, Mayhew played most of his rugby at lock and had more than 10 years in the Northcote senior team. He played his last senior game only three years ago.

When North Harbour was founded Mayhew was one of their union doctors. He says he was fortunate to get in early with the country's newest union and it wasn't too long before he was nominated for the position as All Black doctor.

Abercrombie started off at Otago University doing a dental intermediate but was quickly sidetracked into doing a double major in Speights consumption and snow skiing!

After two years of being sidetracked he headed home to Auckland. After a year of doing odd jobs he took up a family friend's suggestion to try his hand at physiotherapy.

His father — a general practitioner — didn't really know what the future held for physios. But his son "gave it a whirl", starting in 1976 and finishing three years later.

After a brief stint in Auckland Abercrombie headed to Hamilton and was involved with the Waikato team in 1980 — the year the Mooloo men lifted the Ranfurly Shield from Auckland.

Abercrombie then headed to central Canada where he completed a postgraduate course and met his future wife. He worked in Winnipeg for a while and then Calgary for a year before returning to the North Shore in 1983 to set up a practice.

Abercrombie had played some senior rugby and, at rep level, was a hooker in the Auckland under-21 team.

But whereas "Doc" Mayhew is a relative giant, "Abo" stands only 1.70m! He was, he laments, "a wee bit small" for the hurly burly of the front row.

Both "Doc" and "Abo" have family connections in rugby.

Mayhew's younger brother David is locking for North Harbour and was a 1990 All Black trialist.

Abercrombie's father Gibby was a hooker for Scotland in the 1950s. His younger brother Iain was a long serving

Auckland hooker in the late '70s and early '80s. He was even an All Black reserve for the "Baby Blacks" in the test against France at Lancaster Park in 1986.

"New Zealand's a country," says Abercrombie, "where once your family's involved in rugby it's with you for the rest of your life — whether you like it or not!"

Thankfully, Abercrombie and Mayhew have thrived on the rugby environment and they remember playing against each other 20 years ago.

As a Westlake Boys' High School product Abercrombie regularly caught up with Rosmini College's Mayhew on the playing field.

In fact, the pair first played against each other before the youngest current All Black, Wellington's Simon Mannix, was even born!

Because of their rugby background the doctoring duo are well suited to working with the All Black team. And their knowledge of each other and long friendship makes them a real "team".

So how *do* they get on from a work point of view?

"It's not a hierarchical relationship. It's pretty democratic," says Mayhew. "He's short and ugly and doesn't know much about physiotherapy . . . but, apart from that, he's not a bad bloke."

"Yeah," says Abercrombie, "it's a purely platonic relationship . . . definitely not physical!

"From a working point of view we're quite fortunate our individual practices are close to each other. We liaise closely not only with the players we're involved with in the Auckland scene but also on the patients we deal with on a day to day basis.

"It's great from my point of view to ring up John and say I've got someone down here who's been mucked around, the injury's five to seven days old and nothing's been done about it.

"John's great because he invariably sees them straight away and it saves so much time. There *is* a lot of time wasted with some injuries, especially sports injuries where patients may see their general practitioner who takes a very conservative point of view.

"It's not necessarily a wrong approach but it's conservative and he may not appreciate the necessity for that individual to be playing again as quickly as possible.

"So, it's nice that I can get John to hurry things up. His relationship with specialists like orthopaedic surgeons is a

real bonus."

Adds Mayhew: "But not only are we fortunate in working within close proximity of each other, we're also pretty close to the players.

"In the last couple of years the All Black team has been dominated by players from up north and about two-thirds of the team would live within ten miles of our respective practices.

"That's been handy because you're looking after the guys all the time — before, during and after any tour. Because you know them so well and you're dealing with them all the time it makes the job a touch easier."

But it isn't a picnic for the pair by any means. Both have plenty to keep them busy while on tour or during home test matches.

"In a home series we're looking after any injuries that've occurred before coming together in camp and looking after any injuries that occur during the lead-up to the test," Mayhew says.

"For example, Zinzan Brooke's sprained ankle in the lead-up to the third test against Australia in Wellington this year.

"I arranged x-rays and treatment and made the decision on whether he was fit to play or not.

"That can be an anxious time because you have to take into account the player's desire to play and balance that against what's in the best interests of the team.

"It was particularly difficult in Zinny's case because of the similarities with a case the previous year.

"Michael Jones had sprained his ankle in the lead-up to the test against Argentina. That also happened to be in Wellington and there were a couple of other thought-provoking similarities.

"As most people are aware Jones *did* play and that was the test where he damaged his knee so badly.

"Now, his ankle sprain didn't in any way cause the damage to the knee — that was a freak accident — but Grizz still remembered the lead-up and certainly didn't want the same sort of thing happening with Zinny the next day.

"Thankfully, Zinny came through the test well, although he was, like all of us, disappointed in the result."

Doc Mayhew's other responsibilities in camp include arranging food and looking after the diet of the players which, he says, is generally "quite lousy" at times!

He'll liaise with hotel staff about the menu and admits one of his biggest fears is food poisoning, such as the bout which laid low many of the players before the third test against Australia in 1980.

Because he has to cover every eventuality Doc Mayhew takes away enough medical supplies to cover any potential medical problem — not just injuries but illness as well.

He'll arrange vaccinations for the team before tours, trying to stave off the risk of influenza or hepatitis B. Then it's a case of filling his cases!

"On last year's tour to Wales and Ireland I took the equivalent of two average sized suitcases full of medical supplies.

"I probably came back with one still full and the other still containing some supplies.

"But you never know what's required and some things you'll run out of while others you'll hardly touch.

"I take all the standard medical things — antibiotics, anti-inflammatories, surgical equipment like syringes to drain ears. If anyone has a medical problem like asthma or diabetes I'll stock up with medication to treat those.

"And, of course, you end up treating all the media too, so you have to be prepared!"

Abo's bag of tricks is even more imposing size-wise.

"I'd take two suitcases of tape, strapping and bits and pieces like needles for acupuncture," Abercrombie said.

"Then there's electrical equipment like an ultra-sound machine, an interferential and a magnetic therapy unit.

"Throw in another bag with water bottles and the like and add my portable manipulation couch with its adjustable legs and head unit and you can see I have a bit of gear to contend with!"

Abercrombie's routines on tour are basically the same but because different players are suffering different injuries no day is ever the same.

"On a typical day, and match days are different again, I'm generally up around seven o'clock in the morning, have a bite to eat and start treating the first players around a quarter past eight. I'd generally spend an hour and a half doing the basic physio work and strapping players up ready for training.

"John and I generally get involved in training. We do the same things the players do and that gives us a good chance to keep an eye out for those who may be limping or attempting to cover injuries they haven't told us about.

"We're also right there staying on top of anything that might happen on the training field, like guys running into each other as Grant Fox and Matthew Ridge did in Wales last year. Doc had to jump in and start stitching on the spot!

"Following training it's icing down a few of the guys who are carrying minor injuries and then back to the hotel. I often see a few of the guys before lunch if they have something on in the afternoon.

"After grabbing some lunch I'll generally have a bit of the afternoon off. When I say that, I mean away from the team. John and I may go for a wander around the shops or take a look at a gym somewhere. Sometimes, however, you'll have to take one of the players to a specialist.

"Before the evening meal it's a treatment session again in my room. That's repeated after dinner providing there isn't a function to go to. If there is something on we'll attend and those who need treatment will receive it when we get back.

"So the day can stretch to nine at night or, if there's a function on, I could still be working at midnight.

"Match days are quite pleasant because the guys generally get up later. I can spend a bit more time over breakfast because lunch is often missed.

"After reading the newspaper I return to my room and the guys generally wander in and out wanting little things done. Some like to be stretched and there's little routines that I'm part of. Generally, there's hardly ever any treatment itself done on match days.

"Usually by twelve thirty I've strapped all the players who like to get that out of the way before going to the ground. After a team meeting it's on the bus and off to the park. In the changing rooms I'll strap the rest of the guys who need it and help them get stretched.

"From there it's the usual on-field routine."

Says Mayhew: "And that involves making sure the hair is right and he's looking good for the cameras!"

Abercrombie takes the jibe in the good humour it was intended. They understand what makes the other tick and have formed a special bond.

It's a relationship that's needed on tour because there are times when they take a step back and let the players do their own thing. For the most part, however, they're an integral part of the team and just "one of the boys".

"On tour we are treated basically as part of the playing team," said Mayhew. "There's no 'us and them' mentality.

"If you want to train with the guys you'll get rucked or battered about just like anyone else. If they have to do a hundred press-ups, you have to as well. It's either full-on or you don't take part because you can't have the best of both worlds and train just when it suits you.

"I think the players respect that and they'll look after you if you look after them. We do get about quite a bit with them. We've had the odd late night out with the boys!"

"Doc and I see a bit of each other socially at home," said Abercrombie, "and the night before a match is another time where the two of us will often go out by ourselves for a couple of quiet drinks. It's often a late night for us and a chance to relax and unwind. But you also find it's a good time to assess the week and decide what approach to take the next day.

"It's good to get away from the players at times. You need some space, especially after a month or six weeks away on tour."

Adds Mayhew: "That's true because Dave's room is often the social focus of the whole team in a way.

"It's a treatment room but you'll have two or three guys getting treated and another five or six hangers-on who are just watching TV or playing cards. On an average night there may be seven or eight guys in there at a time and different players coming and going."

Abercrombie: "If you look at the night before the third test against Australia in Wellington there would have been about twelve guys in there most of the evening. It's good. It's a place for players to relax."

Mayhew: "Some find it hard to sleep on the night of a big match and it's almost therapy. They can sit down and talk and generally while away those nervous nights."

Abercrombie: "And they *can* be long nights. During a home test everyone stays in the hotel and a lot of them won't go to bed until around eleven o'clock or midnight. They've generally seen all the movies on the in-house video by this stage, so they like to unwind. *And* use my phone for international toll calls!"

Mayhew: "On tour of course you have 'dirty dirties', those not involved in the match the next day as a player or reserve. The ritual is that they go out on the town, leaving those playing to gear up mentally and have a quiet night. Abo and I may often catch up with the 'dirty dirties' at some stage in the night. But in a home test where everyone's involved the players confine themselves to the hotel."

Despite being so close to the team, Mayhew and Abercrombie say there's no problems maintaining their objectivity.

They realise the main reason they're on tour isn't to pack down in scrums at training or provide a room for nervous, card-playing test players on the eve of a big match. They're on tour as medical professionals and have to be honest in their assessment of a player's injury, even if their appraisal isn't what the player wants to hear.

The same goes for socialising with the troops.

"There are advantages in John and I being with the players so long and knowing them extremely well," said Abercrombie.

"There are times when you get a feeling they don't want to be hassled or talked to. When they just want to be left on their own it's something you *do* have a feeling for.

"Conversely, there are times when you also feel they need some help or a bit of a prop from you.

"That was the case with Alan Whetton during his hamstring trouble on the tour of Wales and Ireland. In 'AJ's' case it involved telling him he was a lot better than he perceived himself to be and gearing him mentally to go for a run and test himself.

"We also knew when to pull him back and say to Grizz he wasn't ready for a game and wasn't to be considered.

"I think the guys trust our judgement and respect it."

"We took a bit of a punt with AJ," says Mayhew. "I've heard the criticism that he went back a game too early. We knew he wasn't one hundred per cent but we had to give him the chance to press his claims for the Irish test. As it was, he played pretty well against Ulster after the test against Ireland and I'm sure if he'd been selected in the Barbarians match he would've played superb footy."

Adds Abercrombie: "He only played half a game in his first match back but, really, he came off not because he damaged the hamstring again but because he was a bit sore and didn't want to take too much of a chance with it.

"Most of the guys are pretty sensible. They know what their limits are and few of them would push themselves beyond those limits."

"The bottom line," says Mayhew, "is that we can be one of the boys but we've got to do our professional job. It's all

very well going out on the town with them or training with them but if they perceived we weren't doing the job properly they'd be peeved.

"They get critical of us at times and I'm sure there are times we haven't given the ideal treatment — not through a lack of trying but because we made a misjudgement or whatever. It's just like one of the players taking the wrong option on the field.

"There's a bit of pressure from the management as well. They want what's best for the team and if that means trying to ascertain when a guy's coming

back from a torn hamstring, it's a question they're duty-bound to keep asking. Unfortunately, there's no fool-proof way of telling something like that, so it can be fairly testing at times."

"The criticism and rev-ups we get from the players at times is good from our point of view though," says Abercrombie.

"It makes you realise your place on tour and what you're there for. Really, you're there to work.

"It's nice to be away on tour and see different things and train with the guys. But Doc and I are there to do a job. Anything beyond that is a bonus."

"DOC" and "Abo" assist an injured John Schuster from the field at Swansea in 1989.

Photo by : PETER BUSH

Doc Mayhew will never forget one time on tour when his medical "expertise" was stretched by a panicking All Black.

The embarrassing moment was during the early part of the All Black tour to Australia in 1988 — his first tour with the team.

Because Michael Jones couldn't play in the first test because of his religious beliefs, the in-form Mike Brewer was the All Blacks' openside flanker.

"Bruiser had a knee complaint," Mayhew remembers, "and I gave him an injection which numbed it well and allowed him to get on with the game without thinking about it.

"During the week he trained freely and was picked to play against Queensland at Ballymore the following Sunday.

"Ten minutes before the game he wanted another injection and I said no, we'd talked about it and he didn't need it.

"But Mike was keen to have the jab and, at the last minute, I relented. The team was lining up to go on the field and in the panic I didn't quite inject him in the right place.

"I'd injected too close to one of the nerves that holds the foot up and after ten minutes his foot just dropped dead with temporary paralysis!

"I realised immediately what had happened and Dave went on to the field to see what he could do about it."

"When I got to Mike," Abercrombie continues, "he couldn't lift his foot up and was urging me to strap it up!

"I said there was nothing I could do but he practically begged me to give it a whirl. So, I strapped it up and out like you would for a twisted ankle in the hope it would hold his foot up long enough for the injection to wear out. Then he should've been able to get some circulation back into it and become mobile again.

"But it was like a useless paddle and in the end he had to come off!"

"The most embarrassing thing," says Mayhew, "was that he was named in the team for the next game against Queensland B just a few days later. The media were amazed because the foot had looked so bad when he had to come off.

"In hindsight, I should have just injected water into it because it was too close to the game and whereas before we'd worked out exactly where the injection would be, this time we were in a mild panic.

"It's funny to look back on it now but at the time it was a lesson learnt and I was so embarrassed!"

Mayhew has since "made amends" for putting his foot in it with Brewer, not least in Wales last year when John Kirwan ruptured his achilles tendon.

The fact Kirwan made such a miraculous recovery and played in all the domestic tests the following season was in no small way attributable to Mayhew's pre-tour preparation and his network of medical "advisors".

"Before the Pontypool game JK had a slight pain in his achilles tendon which settled down two days before the game following medication and physiotherapy. In the final two training runs he was as good as gold.

"During the game, as I'm sure most people would know, he ruptured the achilles tendon and Abo made the initial diagnosis on the field which I confirmed when he came off.

"Being in rugby-mad Wales there were thousands of officials and other people milling around under the stand. I was being given advice from all quarters. They're all well-meaning but I didn't know which was the best place to take JK to and wasn't keen to gamble.

"Having worked in London I rang an orthopaedic surgeon friend of mine and explained my predicament. He recommended Greg Jones in Newport, so I then rang Greg and asked if he could look at John.

"The match was still going on when we arrived at the hospital only half an hour later. Within two hours John was being operated on!

"When I first arrived I warned the hospital staff that the place was going to turn into a media circus before you could say 'Bob Deans definitely scored'. They must have been the only Welsh people that weren't rugby-mad because they asked why! Within an hour they had appreciated how famous their patient was. There were media people and cameras everywhere!"

Because the team was staying in Cardiff at that stage and then shifted to Swansea, Mayhew became an expert on driving around Wales.

He commuted to the hospital, sometimes twice a day, to see how Kirwan was and bring a different batch of JK's All Black team mates to see him.

When the commuting stopped with Kirwan's rejoining the team Mayhew was still flat out.

"I was supervising his on-going care at the hotel because we weren't keen on him flying within the first couple of weeks after surgery, especially with his leg in plaster. After that first fortnight JK could easily have returned home but his management skills came in handy on tour and he was still a valued member of the party. Besides, he *had* to stay on. Who else could have done such a great job on the tour video he was helping make!"

Otago loose forward Paul Henderson was another player Mayhew ferried around Wales as he worked on the initial treatment for the openside flyer's knee injury.

Combine that with management duties and the attending of functions and you can see being the team doctor on tour is no lark.

So what *is* the big attraction when one considers the money the pair lose and the time spent away from their families?

"We receive the same daily allowance as the players while on tour," says Abercrombie. "The fact you're not working at home means there's a lot of lost income. I haven't sat down and worked it out but when I return from a tour I'm generally looking at a ten thousand dollar overdraft!"

"If you're looking at it from a monetary point of view," says Mayhew, "you wouldn't bother doing it. I'd hate to think what it costs me a year. Besides the time spent on tour with the All Blacks or North Harbour, I also treat the top players around the region free of charge.

"I enjoy the game though and dealing with the people. The bonus for me is the trips you have away. It's an interesting break from your practice and offers a bit of variety. You're having opportunities and experiences you wouldn't have otherwise.

"So, you lose money but you gain in other areas."

Mayhew and Abercrombie are both keen to retain the positions until after the World Cup at least.

"I believe the NZRFU isn't calling for nominations next year. But that has to be rubber stamped and it's dependant on us doing our jobs well until then," says Abercrombie.

"Again, it's just like a player. We have to keep performing to merit selection.

"The World Cup is also as much a goal for us as it is a player. It wouldn't be a bad time to finish either. All going to plan, I'll have been in the position for four years and it would probably be time for someone else to have a go.

"Both of us have young families and what we're doing means three months-plus away from them. So family and work life does get seriously affected."

Doc Mayhew echoes Abercrombie's comments. Child number four was on its way as the All Black team departed for France. That makes for "a hefty price to pay" for his rugby involvement.

But there's no doubting they'll look back on their time as "honorary" All Blacks with fondness. And while the World Cup will be the pinnacle, Abercrombie has another goal.

"I'd love to go to South Africa," he says. "Every rugby player would like to go and play there. I'm no different in my job. It would be a real highlight to experience the place."

The pair have talked about ways they can continue to contribute to rugby once they've slipped out of their current roles.

"We'd like to look at being appointed to the NZRFU in some way," says Abercrombie.

"We'd like to put something back into the game and not necessarily from a medical point of view. We've seen how other countries run things from coaching to administration. Perhaps we could pass on some ideas through being involved in an advisory capacity."

Their desire to keep working and, hopefully, helping the development of rugby is a measure of the duo's commitment to the sport.

"Like I said earlier, rugby's in our veins!" Abercrombie says.

"My two boys — one aged three, the other only one — are already rugby-minded. The eldest runs around the backyard the whole day with his rugby ball. And we can't get him out of his little All Black jumper.

"That's great from my wife's point of view. She's Canadian and didn't know what the word rugby meant until we met. So, in seven years she's had a pretty good introduction to the New Zealand way of life!"

Knowing the way Abercrombie — and Mayhew — feel about the sport, those seven years will have been but a mere introduction.

Doc and Abo — two of the All Blacks' closest allies and friends — have a lot more to give on the rugby front yet. ∎

JOHN KIRWAN hobbles off at Pontypool after tearing his achilles tendon.
Photo by : PETER BUSH

Dean McLachlan is a radio broadcaster with the Independent Radio Sport network, based in Auckland. He previously worked as a journalist on *Rugby News.*

PROFILE : IAN JONES

Full name: Ian Donald Jones.
Birthdate: April 17, 1967.
Zodiac sign: Aries.
Birthplace: Whangarei.
Residence: Kamo, Whangarei.
Occupation: Company rep.
Height: 1.98m.
Weight: 102kg.
Marital status: Single.
Position: Lock/No 8.
Present club: Kamo.
Most difficult opponent: Anyone who gives 100 per cent.
Best rugby memories: Winning selection for the All Blacks; every game I play for them.
Biggest disappointment: Losing third test versus Australia in Wellington, 1990.
Favourite country: Ireland.
Biggest influence on career: Listening to anyone with something relevant to say.
Other sports/leisure interests: Fishing, swimming, diving, tennis.
Favourite rugby grounds: Okara Park, Kamo Rec.
Favourite films: *Anima! Hours.*
Favourite TV show: *Married With Children.*
Favourite music: Dire Straits.
Favourite food: Home made.
Funniest rugby experience: Alan Whetton's speeches.
Biggest drag in rugby: Inconsistencies.

PROFILE : SIMON MANNIX

Full name: Simon James Mannix.
Birthdate: August 10, 1971.
Zodiac sign: Leo.
Birthplace: Lower Hutt.
Residence: Lower Hutt.
Occupation: Student.
Height: 1.76m.
Weight: 77kg.
Marital status: Single.
Position: First-five.
Present club: Petone.
Most difficult opponent: The next one.
Best rugby memory: Winning selection for the All Blacks.
Biggest disappointment: Each loss.
Favourite country: New Zealand.
Biggest influence on career: My family.
Other sports/leisure interests: Surfing, golf, cricket, tennis, swimming, skiing.
Favourite rugby ground: Eden Park.
Favourite films: *Tango, Cash.*
Favourite TV shows: *Cheers, Tour of Duty.*
Favourite music: McHammer.
Favourite food: Italian.
Funniest rugby experience: Training runs when we tackled tyres and then ran with them above our heads.
Biggest drag in rugby: Uninformed critics.

PROFILE : MIKE BREWER

Full name: Michael Robert Brewer.
Birthdate: November 6, 1964.
Zodiac sign: Scorpio.
Birthplace: Pukekohe.
Residence: Dunedin.
Occupation: Promotions manager for Eadie Bros (NZ) Ltd.
Height: 1.95m.
Weight: 99kg.
Marital status: Single.
Position: No 8/flanker.
Present club: Kaikorai.
Previous club: University.
Most difficult opponents: Dale Atkins, Brent Pope.
Best rugby memory: My first test against France in 1986.
Biggest disappointment: First test loss against Australia, 1986 at Athletic Park.
Favourite countries: Ireland, Australia.
Biggest influence on career: All coaches.
Other sports/leisure interests: Golf, tennis, the beach, water sports; music; cooking.
Favourite rugby ground: Carisbrook, Dunedin.
Favourite films: None especially.
Favourite TV shows: Sports shows, news.
Favourite music: Van Morrison, blues.
Favourite food: Italian; Indian.
Funniest rugby experience: Knowing Brent Pope.
Biggest drag in rugby: Injuries; after-match functions.

PROFILE : TERRY WRIGHT

Full name: Terence John Wright.
Birthdate: January 21, 1963.
Zodiac sign: Aquarius.
Birthplace: Auckland.
Residence: Mt Eden, Auckland.
Occupation: Accountant/auditor for Ernst & Young.
Height: 1.78m.
Weight: 79kg.
Marital status: Engaged to Lindsay and getting married December 1990.
Position: Wing/fullback.
Present club: Auckland Marist.
Previous club: Northcote.
Most difficult opponent: Patrice Lagisquet.
Best rugby memories: First test versus France 1986; winning Ranfurly Shield off Canterbury 1985; winning Gallaher Shield final 1989.
Biggest disappointment: Playing for New Zealand sevens in Sydney tournament 1986 and not going on to Hong Kong with the rest of the team.
Favourite country: New Zealand.
Biggest influence on career: My father.
Other sports/leisure interests: Fishing, diving, golf.
Favourite rugby ground: Eden Park.
Favourite film: *Top Gun.*
Favourite TV show: *LA Law.*
Favourite music: Anything except rap.
Favourite food: Lindsay's spagtagne (mixture of lasagne and spaghetti).
Funniest rugby experience: Watching Zinzan Brooke play golf on tour.
Biggest drag in rugby: Wet days when the wings get forgotten.

CLINTON 6:30 A.M.

UNCLE JOE'S A REAL DAGG

LOCK UP YOUR DAUGHTERS, THE BOYS ARE IN TOWN

7:30 AM MOSGIEL ... DAD SAID PUMPING UP THE FLAT TYRE WOULD BE GOOD TRAINING FOR A FUTURE ALL BLACK. UNCLE JOE SAID IT WAS ONLY FLAT ON THE BOTTOM.

7:30 A.M. I SAT IN THE CAR-PARK WHILE DAD AND UNCLE JOE TOPPED UP THE SUPPLIES

10:30 AM. WE WALKED TO CARISBROOK WITH 41,538 OTHERS UNCLE JOE SAID I MADE IT 41,538½ .... HE'S A LAUGH MY UNCLE

It takes ALL THREE!

It's PURITY, BODY and FLAVOUR that makes CROWN CHAMPION consistently the most popular of ales!

12:01 P.M.

N°1 GATE

BURNS ST

GRANDSTAND • ENCLOSURE

CHILDREN

ADULT

WE'LL WAIT IN-SIDE FOR YOU

12:20 PM WHILE I WAITED FOR DAD AND UNCLE JOE.. I GOT IN SOME SUPPLIES...HOT PIES AND LANE'S SUNSHINE SOFT-DRINKS

AHHH

2C

C4

JOHN HART'S
GUIDE TO TALENT SPOTTING

By HEATHER KIDD

Teenage talent is something New Zealanders get excited about and more especially when the "wonderkid" is a rugby player. We all enjoy the rags-to-riches type story of an unknown bursting through to the big time.

In recent years there have been plenty of such stories to tell and one of the best would be the tale of the young butcher's apprentice who was plucked from Auckland third grade rugby and deposited, as a surprise selection, in the Auckland A team to play a President's XV in a special pre-season match.

John Kirwan was just 18-years-old in 1983 when Auckland selector-coach John Hart picked him for his Auckland team.

There was nothing rash about Hart's decision to bring Kirwan up to representative rugby. The previous year he'd heard mention of a talented Marist fifth grader so on his way to a match he detoured to watch Kirwan play.

He was, Hart recalls, big and raw but his talent was apparent.

"He expressed himself well with his enthusiasm and his skills and I could tell he had a feel for the game which is an important factor."

Kirwan didn't know it then but Hart had his eye on him and the following year he watched him play again. This time Hart was more specific about what he wanted. To develop the style of play he wanted, Hart was seeking strong running wings and in Kirwan he saw the type of player who could give him what he required.

The second game Hart saw reinforced his earlier views of Kirwan. The teenager showed more maturity and his game had also improved.

"He did things that appealed. He beat people with good body swerves and he showed an ability to hold on to the ball in the tackle. He was strong."

Hart was certain Kirwan could become an integral part of his Auckland team but he chose to approach with caution. First he spoke to Kirwan's parents and told them that their son possessed considerable rugby talents and that he was thinking of including him in the Auckland squad for the centennial matches.

Then he told them a white lie. He said he was considering playing Kirwan in the B team which would play the Vice-President's XV when, in fact, he intended using him in the A side.

In hindsight it was a wise move. Kirwan's parents, Hart says, were "shocked and surprised". They chatted for a while then Hart had a brief talk with Kirwan himself, although not about his intentions to include him in the Auckland team.

It was Kirwan's parents who mentioned to the young player that Hart was keen to promote him and only after that did Hart get Kirwan up to his office to talk seriously about rugby.

Hart's skills at managing people are well documented and they are one of the reasons for his outstanding success, particularly in developing young rugby talent. It is, he says, a big decision to take a young player and transpose him to a totally different environment.

"You don't want to push him to a stage where you upset his personal development," he warns.

With Kirwan he had few worries. He'd checked his background and from their meetings ascertained that Kirwan was "a good kid who could handle the situation if it was managed well. He was a bit shy initially but as he relaxed he gained confidence and spoke with a lot of maturity."

Hart continued to give the impression

JOHN HART in earnest discussion with Graham Williams, the former All Black and his assistant coach on the 1990 New Zealand Colts tour of Australia.

Photo by : PETER BUSH

he wanted Kirwan for the B team and that he'd selected him to represent the youth of Auckland and therefore his inclusion in the squad would not be viewed as permanent.

His reasoning was double-edged. If Kirwan failed to measure up he could return to third grade with his pride intact. If, as Hart had correctly assumed, Kirwan would be a success, he could include him in the squad and no pressure had been put upon the young player.

Hart knew that it would be to Kirwan's advantage to play in the A team. There he would be surrounded by good and experienced players who could help and protect the novice.

The coach rang one of his team, Gary Cunningham, and asked him to keep an eye on his young protege. Cunningham did just that. He took Kirwan to trainings and roomed with him when the team stayed together.

Eventually all the planning, talking and training was put to the test. Kirwan played his first game for the Auckland As and his side won 42–7. More importantly, Kirwan came through the encounter with flying colours.

He came close to scoring a try, he did what was asked of him. To Hart the teenager was still raw but he was keen and he was on his way.

It was a fairytale year for Kirwan in what was a somewhat disappointing season for Auckland. None of the team was named in the All Blacks who were to tour England and Scotland at the end of the season.

Kirwan ended the year as Auckland's top tryscorer. He touched down seven times although, ironically, only one of those tries was scored on Eden Park and that was in Auckland's 25–7 win over Counties.

Interestingly, one other Auckland try-scorer that day was Wayne Shelford.

Kirwan was selected for the North Island team in 1983 and also made the New Zealand Colts team. His days as a third grader were well behind him.

But, says Hart, that hasn't made Kirwan sit back and relax. With Hart's guidance Kirwan learned to analyse his game because as Hart so rightly states there is really only one person who knows how well you've played and that, of course, is yourself.

"It's very important for players to sit down in the dressing room after each game and take, say thirty seconds, to think about the last eighty minutes. You can pat yourself on the back for things done well but also look at things that didn't go so well and then go out and work at nullifying those weaknesses or failings.

"John really practised what I suggested as he grew up in '84 and '85. Perhaps, sometimes, he is over-critical of himself nowadays.

"I recall he scored a great try in the North versus South match in 1985 and I went to see him afterwards and congratulated him on his performance. But he was worried about why he'd dropped an up-and-under.

"At the All Black trials in Hamilton in 1984 he scored three tries and it was there I'd say his star was born. I again told him he'd played well. He wanted to know why Bernie Fraser had beaten him in the corner."

Hart isn't suggesting Kirwan can't accept compliments. What he is saying is that there are always lessons to be learned. According to Hart there are a lot of JK's in the world, plenty of kids with talent, but for individuals to succeed they must do what John Kirwan does — make the most of opportunities and work hard at developing skills and fitness.

As the New Zealand Colts coach, Hart sees many talented players. But physical skills aren't everything. Hart puts a lot of emphasis on an individual's personality and for very good reasons.

"Rugby is a team game and sport, to me, is one way to teach people how to develop. All the things that are important in society can be found in playing a team sport — how to work on relationships, respecting other people, your team mates and the opposition.

"Rugby is a sport which accommodates all body types — fat, skinny, slow kids and fast ones.

THE youthful (18-year-old) John Kirwan as he was in 1983 when John Hart "spotted" him.
Photo by : PETER BUSH

"Individual sports aren't bad but I think team sports are better in assisting personal development. Team sports help a person realise they can't win on their own and that they have to get help from others. When the emphasis is on individual success it can lead to more selfish attitudes.

"The right balance probably contains a mixture of both team and individual sport."

Individual brilliance, New Zealand Colts players soon learn under Hart, is not enough. Prior to the team assembling before a tour Hart has made it his business to find out a little about most of the aspirants and he sets much store on personality.

"I have to know if they will fit into the team. Touring is often the making of players and they learn the disciplines necessary — travelling, training, preparing for games, being coached and hopefully learning new things about their own game and the team plan.

"Colts rugby is the hardest category to coach. In this year's team we had All Blacks and we also had six or seven players who'd never played above senior club level. We are trying to get everyone to the same level over a two week period."

The boys, Hart says, very quickly become men. And not all the men will make it to the top. Luck still plays a part in rugby selections and Hart says never underestimate that factor.

But there are rules to follow if you want to succeed. Be a team player because, after all, rugby is a game with 15 in each side. Learn to take pressure and work at applying yourself 100 per cent.

According to Hart it's the mental hardness that fails some people. They can go for 70 minutes out on the rugby paddock but can't sustain concentration for that final, and often very vital, last 10 minutes.

These days there are more pressures on young people, more recreational choices, more worries about finding employment.

"In my day there were no cars and the first fifteen was everything," Hart says. "It is certainly different today but the rewards are greater if you get there. But it won't be easy. You've got to want it from the heart, not just the lips. You've got to learn to take the knocks, learn to take advice and be prepared to go out and ask for it.

"It's important to have fun. If you're not enjoying it you'll never get there.

"It's important to be a good loser and it's important to be a good reserve.

"You will only play as well as you train. You take your training out on the field with you.

"It's also important to know how to prepare for a game. There's no single way of doing it but unless you learn to sit down and think about the game beforehand you will fail."

John Kirwan is a superb example of how one young man, with natural talents, made the most of the opportunities that came his way. His development was helped by the guiding hand of John Hart but the final responsibility, the desire to succeed, could only come from Kirwan himself.

Now a senior member of the All Black side Kirwan has never stopped asking questions about his own performance. When a serious injury forced him out of last year's All Black tour to Wales and Ireland he had to work long and hard to make it back to full fitness.

He, and Hart, knows what it takes to be an All Black. It takes a lot. ■

JOHN HART . . . his skills at managing people are well documented.

Heather Kidd as the assistant editor of *Rugby News* became the first woman to be attached to major international touring teams. A novelist and successful journalist she was named New Zealand sports writer of the year for 1990. She currently lives in Limerick, Ireland, where her husband is rugby coaching.

RUGBY'S A FUNNY OLD GAME

By KEITH QUINN

Let no one ever say a rugby reporter's job is boring or dull. In fact being a rugby reporter is often quite the opposite. It's a job that often requires the reporter to have a roaring sense of humour. That way he or she can get through the most amusing of situations or wade one's way through colourful stories from rugby's past. That's what I hope this story might be, a trip through some of rugby's interesting and unusual situations and memories. Let rugby trivia reign!

Believe me, although rugby can be, and is, the most serious of pastimes for most of its participants, the curious and funny angles in the many stories which surround the history of the game are always worth a smile in the retelling.

Take the field the game is played on. To have a game of rugby football we assume that all playing surfaces bear some semblance of being uniform in size and shape.

I mean, that's basic isn't it? But throughout the rugby world one of the most interesting factors to observe are the varied conditions under which a game is played.

But it doesn't matter what the conditions are like; rain, hail or sunshine, rugby is worth playing anywhere, anytime with anyone.

In one experience this writer had in 1990 there was the contrast between reporting international rugby at Eden Park in Auckland and then only days later doing the same job at Rugby Park in Greymouth.

The Auckland ground is modern sophistication itself; a wide expanse of seating at each end with towering goalposts, an electronic scoreboard, ground staff numbering dozens to lovingly manicure the turf and offices, restaurants and social areas in the imposing grandstands to either side of the field.

Above the stands the sponsors' boxes are serviced by uniformed men and women with all the deference of a bygone age of gentility.

To reach the lofty perch of one of those boxes to enjoy the champagne and hors-d'oeuvres, or to travel beyond to the television commentary position one has to produce a ticket, show it to a security guard and ride up in a silent lift.

At Greymouth, on the other hand, there is only one small building that could be called a sideline grandstand. It has no actual seats in it, the "Coasters" plonk their backsides down on the bare boards. The structure could hold, maybe, 200 people only. There are flimsy dressing rooms underneath and if one wants to film a game from the roof for TV the first stop is the groundsman's potting shed to borrow his ladder!

Despite the obvious differences in the above contrast, the game of rugby is the thing that binds New Zealand together.

The differences become akin to the spirit. And that spirit means a good reporter could perhaps smile at the lack of sophistication on the West Coast while recognising that in many ways, with its simplicity, the Greymouth ground has many advantages over the complicated city slickers of the north.

Rugby has always been that way. There have always been the Eden Parks, the Twickenhams and the Murrayfields, those smooth stadia which ooze confidence and money, but I'll bet those who played in the first ever game of rugby between Fiji and Samoa in 1926 did not worry about the condition of the ground — even though there was a large tree growing in the field of play at around the 22 metre line!

The players merely played around the tree, presumably using it in their tactical planning. Why should they have worried about it? After all, at the final whistle they had had a jolly good game of the game we all love. And that's the important thing.

That game, incidentally, kicked off at 7.00am which is perhaps the earliest time an international was ever started. As the game was played on a work day the home Samoan players were able to go to work afterwards and not have their pay docked! Rugby cares about the family, see?

Talking about days of the week, the old days of rugby games only being played on Saturdays are now long gone.

Tests have been played on every day of the week. The All Blacks have played on a Friday at least twice, indeed the Rugby World Cup kicked off on a Friday with the All Blacks playing Italy.

In the early days of the Five Nations championship there was traditionally play on New Year's Day so that meant full test matches on Mondays, Tuesdays, Thursdays etc.

Wales' first international in France was played on Shrove Tuesday. The first international on a Sunday was New Zealand versus Australia at Ballymore in Brisbane in 1968.

The France versus Ireland match in Cork in 1913 had a unique kick-off time. The game started in the morning — on a Monday so that the players could all go to the Easter horse races in the afternoon!

And while there have been tests played in front of huge crowds (the world record is 95,000 for South Africa versus British Isles in Johannesburg in 1955) there was once an international played a day ahead of its advertised date with no crowd watching at all.

It was South Africa versus USA in 1981.

For political reasons the game was switched to a suburban ground and was played simply for the benefit of the players and for the record books. South Africa won comfortably enough on a field that was not marked out properly and had only makeshift goalposts.

Politics were forgotten on one occasion during the Boer War in South Africa in 1899–1902.

Apparently a tough battle had been raging between the rival forces, the British and the Boers, when the commander of the Boers suddenly felt a rugby match should be played.

So he wrote a letter to the British commander.

The letter is in the South African Rugby Board museum. The English translation of the letter, addressed to the Hon Major Edwards and sent to General SG Maritz of the Transvaal Scouting Corps, reads thus: "I wish to inform you that I have agreed to a rugby match taking place between you and us.

"I, from my side, will agree to a cease-fire tomorrow afternoon from 12 o'clock until sunset. The time and venue of the match to be arranged by you in consultation with Messrs Roberts and van Rooyen, who I am sending to you."

So rugby can stop wars — sometimes!

You see, I'm into my stride now, on these stories and trivia stuff. Rugby is full of it. I like reading about the unusual or amusing.

For instance, answer this. What method did referee Tom Schofield use to straighten up the scrums in the England versus Ireland match in 1914?

Apparently twisting scrums were so much of a problem in the game referee Schofield became exasperated and began kicking the backsides of the No 8 forwards to bring the scrums around!

All this happened at the hallowed Twickenham and caused quite a stir, especially when the same referee, a Welshman, had a long and well-reported dislike of rough play!

Then there have been the characters; Harry Garrett, a Scottish international who played a full international without boots on. It was his specialty — he never even wore socks, let alone shinpads!

And Andre Behoteguy, the French international of the 1920s, played all his internationals wearing a black beret.

Billy Wallace and George Gillett of the 1905 All Blacks sometimes wore sunhats on that tour to keep the sun out of their eyes.

Didier Camberabero, the brilliant French flyhalf of modern times, wears a hairpiece to cover a sensitive feeling he has about his balding head.

GEORGE GILLET, *resplendent in hat, attempting a conversion for the 1905 All Blacks against Devon.*

Basil Maclean, the Irish international, who played against the 1905 All Blacks for four different teams, used to play wearing white kid gloves.

There's even a story about an international from England who used to play wearing a monocle. Gad sir, well done, old chap!

And what about New Zealand rugby trivia? It abounds, I can assure you. Our darkest day in rugby was surely 1949 when, on September 3, our beloved All Blacks lost two tests on the same day.

This true story came about because of a quirk in the organised internationals of that year. New Zealand had resumed its sporting contact with South Africa that year, touring to the republic for the first time in 21 years.

That team took away the 30 best players in New Zealand but those staying at home had to face an Australian touring team.

The Aussies were at full international strength so it was deemed that the tests with the "remainder" All Blacks would be classed as full official tests. So it transpired that each tour scheduled a test for September 3.

Athletic Park in Wellington was the venue for the New Zealand versus Australia test, the first of two they were to play that day.

Thirty-two thousand fans turned up but Australia won by 11–6.

Presumably the crowds then went home to rest before getting up in the night to listen in to Winston McCarthy's radio commentary from far away South Africa.

Durban was the venue for the third test between the Springboks and the All Blacks. But the All Blacks had little luck there either, South Africa creeping to a 9–3 win.

Presumably there were some sad Kiwis who went to bed that morning, two All Black teams had lost test matches on the same day.

In fact, file 1949 as the worst year the All Blacks ever had. In all, they played six tests that year, four in South Africa and two at home against Australia — and the All Blacks lost the whole six!

One of my favourite stories of New Zealand rugby occurred in 1959 when Auckland won the Ranfurly Shield off Southland.

It was the game that turned out to be the great triumph for Fred Allen as the Auckland coach.

Auckland won 13–9 and apparently went out afterwards on a much deserved celebration.

Their next game was to be in Christchurch so they headed there via Queenstown where they were to stay the night. A couple of the lads in the Auckland team adjourned to a nearby pub where a couple of the locals asked them about the Ranfurly Shield.

"It's back at our hotel," said one of the Aucklanders, who were soon persuaded by the locals to go back and get the Shield so they could see this famous log o' wood. The trophy had apparently never before passed through Queenstown.

So the Aucklanders soon returned with the Ranfurly Shield and the team's good fortune was toasted a number of times, while everyone gazed in awe at the great trophy, sitting right there in their very own pub.

Soon a couple of the locals, seeing the Auckland players in action on the bar room snooker table, asked if they could challenge them in a game.

"Sure," said the Aucklanders, in their confident mood, adding, "Why don't we play the snooker match with the Ranfurly Shield at stake?"

So they did and, yes, you guessed it, the locals won the Ranfurly Shield! They won it in a snooker match!

And what's more, the local players won easily each time the increasingly desperate Aucklanders challenged again to get it back.

WHEN Fiji and Tonga first played each other in 1926 there was a large tree growing on the field!

In the end, the city slickers of the Auckland team left the hotel and went back to their own to get some stronger snooker players from the remainder of their rugby team to come back with them to play.

Eventually the better players prevailed and the Ranfurly Shield went to Christchurch with the Aucklanders but in Queenstown, those who remember, can always tell you about the time they won the Ranfurly Shield and defended it stoutly, on a snooker table in a pub, for several hours!

As you might have guessed there is an allowance in that story for exaggeration and that is also one of the great things about rugby. Stories from the old days actually are getting better in the re-telling as the years go by.

But there's another of my favourites which the locals who know best will tell you contains no exaggeration at all.

It concerns the Mercury Bay Rugby Club, the club from that charming little seaport on the Coromandel Coast. Mercury Bay is a small town today but in 1924 it must have been tiny. Yet, according to local legend in that year their little rugby club became the champions of the world.

Follow the logic on this one; it's good!

Here's how it happened: In that year there was an All Black team to be picked to play in Australia then go on to tour the United Kingdom. They visited Australia first and on the return they played and lost to Auckland by 14-3. Several weeks later Auckland travelled south to Thames to play the local sub-union team. In a major upset Thames won, sending the shocked Aucklanders home nursing their wounded rugby prides.

The Thames team meantime showed their vulnerability by losing their next match to Coromandel. The Coromandel team then played their near neighbours, Mercury Bay, who won handsomely.

It was only when the New Zealand All Blacks later toured the world and stayed unbeaten against everybody that some local wag picked up on the earlier sequence of wins and declared Mercury Bay to be the world champions of rugby!

There are also the trick questions of New Zealand rugby. Try these out:

When did Stu Wilson play for the British Isles against the All Blacks?

When did Eric Tindall play for Australia at rugby?

When did Kirwan play on the wing against the All Blacks?

When did the All Blacks win soccer's Chatham Cup?

Who were the tallest All Black team ever to leave New Zealand?

The answers of course contain some quirks about more than one footballer having the same name.

The Stu Wilson who played for the British Isles was actually Stewart Wilson of Scotland who toured New Zealand as a fullback in 1966.

The Eric Tindall was an Australian, with a name spelt slightly different to New Zealand's champion sportsman of the 1930s, Eric Tindill. The Australian, Tindall, had one test for his country in 1973, as a halfback.

The Kirwan who played against the All Blacks as a winger was Gerry Kirwan who appeared for Victoria against the 1968 New Zealand team on their tour of Australia.

The All Blacks who won the prestigious soccer trophy, the Chatham Cup, were actually the Millerton All Blacks, a team of coal miners from the Buller region who took the trophy in consecutive years in the early 1930s.

And the tallest All Black team ever to leave New Zealand? Why, the Harlem Globetrotters heading home, that's who!

Yes, give me rugby for a great game, some outrageous stories, and your humour will never die. ∎

Keith Quinn is a sports journalist with Television New Zealand who has won international acclaim as a TV rugby commentator. He is the author of several books on the sport.

PROFILE : GARY WHETTON

Full name: Gary William Whetton.

Birthdate: December 15, 1959.

Zodiac sign: Sagittarius.

Birthplace: Auckland.

Residence: Northcote Point, Auckland.

Occupation: Sales manager.

Height: 1.98m.

Weight: 108kg.

Marital status: Married to Jane.

Children: William (one-year-old).

Position: Lock.

Present club: Grammar Old Boys.

Previous clubs: West Hartlepool (England), Treviso (Italy).

Most difficult opponent: Andy Haden.

Best rugby memory: Debut for All Blacks 1981 third test against the Springboks.

Biggest disappointment: Missing 1983 All Blacks tour to England and Scotland through injury.

Favourite country: South Africa.

Biggest influence on career: My family, brother AJ, wife Jane.

Other sports/leisure interests: Tennis, scuba diving, golf.

Favourite rugby ground: Eden Park.

Favourite music: Most music except "Rap".

Favourite food: Seafood, curries, steak.

Funniest rugby experience: Joe Stanley trying to kick a football.

Biggest drag in rugby: Weather; time away from family, job, friends outside rugby.

PROFILE : NICK FARR-JONES

Full name: Nicholas Campbell Farr-Jones.

Birthdate: April 18, 1962.

Zodiac sign: Aries.

Birthplace: Sydney.

Residence: Sylvania, Sydney.

Occupation: Solicitor.

Height: 1.78m.

Weight: 85kg.

Marital status: Married to Angela.

Years playing rugby: 16.

Position: Halfback.

Present club: Sydney University.

Most difficult opponent: Jerome Gallion (France).

Best rugby memory: Beating Wales at Cardiff Arms in 1984.

Most memorable matches: Versus New Zealand at Auckland in 1986 and again in Wellington, 1990.

Biggest disappointment: Losing to England in England in 1988.

Favourite country: Argentina.

Biggest influence on career: Michael Hawker.

Other sports/leisure interests: Tennis, golf, snow skiing.

Favourite rugby ground: Twickenham.

Favourite films: *Caddy Shack*, *Butch Cassidy and the Sundance Kid*.

Favourite TV show: *Wide World of Sport*.

Favourite music: Talking Heads, Midnight Oil.

Favourite food: Fresh lobster.

Funniest rugby experience: Seeing Tom Lawton score two tries versus Scotland.

Biggest drag in rugby: Uninformed critics.

THE RUGBY DICTIONARY

By JIM WEBSTER

A B C D E F
G H I J K L
M N O P Q R
S T U V W X
Y Z

A

Abuse Turns defeat into victory.

Advantage The advantage law is more often applied when the referee wants a date with your captain's sister.

After-match functions The officials take over from the players and hand out ties and make speeches to which the players don't listen.

All Blacks Unsavoury types. They've largely pilfered rugby from the Poms. The name and uniform symbolise their opponents' deep depression.

Arms Park A sacred site in Wales for visiting New Zealanders since 1905. Any rugby player who has lost a limb in battle can store it here for safe-keeping.

Arthritis An affliction normally developed late in one's playing career and attacking the right elbow. Medical opinion suggests that drinking through a straw would otherwise prevent it.

Autobiography Mandatory for famous players on retirement. Contains photograph of said hero in short pants as well as one of wife and family, criticism of officials, a World XV in which he selects himself, a tit-bit of sensationalism to assist the sales and a neat list of figures at the end of the book detailing his career stats. Makes an excellent door-stopper.

Autograph A star player practising to become illegible. Many of them become dcotors.

Aye As in "Aye ref, what's that flippin' penalty for?"

B

Ball boy The boy on the touchline with balls under each arm.

Bandage As common in rugby as talkative half-backs. Never worn on the knee which actually hurts but on the "good" knee so as to fool any opposing players who might have evil intent. This means that the "bad" knee has no support and therefore never gets better.

Beer Persistent rumours suggest that the brewers of this amber fluid actually conceived the game of rugby football and not William Webb Ellis at all.

Best and fairest Competitions organised by clubs and newspapers to determine which player has gouged, sworn, punched, trodden and kicked less than anyone else in the team. Usually won by threequarters.

Bidet Used in France for washing mud from boots after a game.

Boots More ceremonial than anything else. Nobody has been able to satisfactorily explain why rugby can't be played in bare feet. Except that when players retire they would not have anything to (1) throw away, (2) burn, or (3) store in a cupboard until they either go mouldy or the fourth XV finds itself short of players one afternoon.

Breakaway Best-known of them is rugby league.

Canadian rugby The worst thing that can happen to a rugby player in Great Britain and Ireland, New Zealand, Australia, South Africa and France is to be transferred in his job to somewhere in the world other than these countries. There have been stories of these lost souls trying to organise matches on the lower slopes of Mt Everest or on an island in the middle of the Zambesi River. The luckier ones have finished up in Canada which is reportedly quite civilised and they have organised their rugby so well that Canada is now one of the better-known outposts of the game. One local custom if the ref isn't any good is to simply dump him on an iceberg and push him out to sea with just his law book for company. This has led to a shortage of referees in Canada.

Cantankerous Used by writers to describe battered old forwards who have played one season too many.

Caps A cap, made of velvet and appropriately inscribed, is awarded on the occasion of a player's first appearance for his national team. At times they have been found to be too small for the swollen head for which they were intended. Most helpful when a player has to go cap-in-hand anywhere.

Captain The player (1) whose father is chairman of selectors, or (2) whose mother washes the team jerseys each Saturday night.

Cauliflower ears A trade union membership card.

Centre As in nerve centre, he is supposed to be in the middle of all the action. However, if the forwards and halves decide to play what is commonly referred to as 10-man rugby then he becomes a dead centre.

Chairman of selectors The one who accepts blame for all the mistakes.

Choice of ends When the captain tries to decide whether to run uphill first or downhill.

Club doctors Ex-players who entered the medical profession and have returned to help the old club in an honorary capacity. The only problem is that they mostly become gynaecologists and obstetricians.

Coach A man who walks into his house at the close of the rugby season and his children say, "Hullo mister, what's your name?" Coaches are seldom home, seldom happy and seldom satisfied.

Coin Tossed in the air by the referee before the game starts to determine if the opposing captains have flexible neck muscles.

Corner post Hard to follow, as are so many things in rugby. These posts don't have corners to them at all.

Dad Soon after birth an infant boy first realises the problems ahead of him when a weeny pair of rugby boots is deposited at the end of his cot, together with a copy of *Rugby Skills for the Beginner* and a small football. Dad will not rest from that day forth until you are capped for your country. The fact that you experience great difficulty making the reserves' bench for your house XV does not deter him. He knows you deserve much better than that and delights in telling the school principal so.

Day, not your You have just been defeated 48–3, the team's champion centre threequarter has broken down and there's no hot water in the dressing shed.

Deadball line A succession of deceased footballs.

Defeat When there are less officials and supporters in the dressing shed after the game than there were before it.

Disinterest When the wingers hear the coach begin his team talk before the game with, "Okay lads, we're going to play it nice and tight today . . . "

Dive, taking a An age-old ploy for gaining much needed rest, or so the halfback can retie his loose bootlace, or the captain can figure out how to overcome the 42-point deficit. A designated player swoons like a Hollywood starlet at which point medical attendants rush on to the pitch and show their talents by treating him for a malady which doesn't exist. When the rest of the team is right to go again, he instantly recovers.

Dog   Usually black and nondescript. Runs on to the field just as the goalkicker is lining up his shot at goal. If the crowd yells at him he has been known to relieve himself on the goalposts or even on the leg of the referee. No one ever confesses to being his master. Runs off again after a few minutes. It's hard to convince non-rugby people that this incident is not devised to provide added excitement to the game.

Donnybrook   When players can't agree.

Dressing shed   Where clothes and comfort are left behind.

Drop kick   Should you miss the ball when attempting to punt it, this affords you a second chance after it hits the ground. If the ball passes accidentally between the goalposts you are awarded three points. Nobody ever tries it on purpose because it's too hard.

Dropout   The rugby blue from Oxford or Cambridge who winds up doing his thesis on violence on the rugby field.

Dummy   (1) The act of shaping to throw a pass and then forgetting to do so. (2) Spat out by a player on the losing team who thinks success transcends enjoyment. (3) Your team mate who has just dropped a pass with the goalline unguarded.

Dummy scissors   A very tricky movement in which nobody quite knows what's happening except the player carrying the ball. Sometimes even he's not too sure. Forwards wisely stay clear of them.

Effort   What the coach always suggests at half-time is considerably lacking.

Ella Ella Ella   Hiccups which occur when watching Aussie rugby.

Embarrassment   (1) You replace your torn shorts in midfield and suddenly recall having forgotten to wear your supports underneath. (2) The opposition finally reaches a century of points and the game has to be stopped while the scoreboard attendant rushes off to get an extra batch of numbers.

End-of-season tour   A post-mortem and a strategy meeting for next season rolled into one.

Ex-player   The pest with the stained club tie, bent nose and cauliflower ears who tells you later in the bar the correct way you should have done things out there today. Somewhere during the conversation he usually says, "I remember a game back in '53 when . . . "

Extra   Extra lap of the oval. Usually reserved by coaches for tubby front row forwards who have been found hiding in the loo during warm-up at training.

Fair catch   The good looking blonde you've picked up in the clubrooms after the game.

False teeth   Most forwards acquire them along the way, like grey hair and arthritic knees. Many wives and girlfriends have said they didn't know their men friends had them until they played rugby (only on the pitch did they take on the appearance of gummy babies). Years ago, before an international match, the teams were to be introduced to a member of the Royal family. It was suggested that those with false teeth should wear them for the occasion. Afterwards the teeth were collected in a bag. Officials could not have foreseen the confusion when the match was over, with forwards from both teams trying on various dentures until they found the right ones.

Five-eighth   Does not play between the four-eighth and six-eighth as you might imagine. In fact, those two positions don't exist. (But in New Zealand they do have a first-five and a second-five!) Best just to call him outside half, flyhalf or "hey you!".

Flanker   Flashy type of player. He stays well out on the flanks during the game but close to the female ones in the clubrooms later.

Football   The object which the laws determine is necessary for a game of rugby, although some games have happily proceeded for several minutes before anyone noticed the ball was missing. Whoever makes them has a lot to answer for, as they never go in the intended direction. Often jaunty wingers find them as slippery as a cake of soap when there is an extra man in the backline and the opposition is in grand disarray.

FALSE TEETH

Garryowen A rugby club in Limerick, Ireland, with a great tradition. Fullbacks wish it had never been founded, for it was from here that emerged "The Garryowen" — the high-lofted punt supported by a rampaging forward pack. The eight forwards, all mean and snarling, arrive at the opposing fullback at precisely the moment he catches the ball. At this point it is wise for spectators to look away.

Genius Your description of the opposing player who has just comprehensively beaten you on the outside and scored the match winning try under the goalposts.
See Quick.

Girlfriends *See* Wives.

Goalline The line over which the opposition seems to have so little trouble crossing. You cannot reliably say whether their goalline even exists.

Goalposts Allegedly 5.6 metres apart but any goal-kicker will tell you this is an absolute lie. They are much closer together than that.

Grandstand Where the experts are.

Grass What is missing from the patch of ground where the largest forward from the opposing team has just tackled you, from behind, with the force of a runaway tank.

Grease Applied to knees and eyebrows before a game to prevent scrapes and gashes and thus also to the hand of the dignitary being introduced to you before the match.

Groundsman The person who seems quite incapable of doing anything about the ridged, barren area of earth in the middle of the ground.

Grubber kick Although grub is a common enough word, meaning tucker, nosh, repast, pickings, nourishment or victuals, a grubber kick does not mean kicking-off straight after lunch. It is a kick which keeps close to the ground like a grub, providing the opposition with food for thought.

Guest speaker An ingenious way of occupying the time between dessert and coffee at annual dinners.

Forfeit The excuse the opposing team offers when it (1) is short of players, (2) has forgotten the jerseys, (3) has caught sight of the size of your team's forwards, or (4) has found the log fire in the local much too warm to leave.

Foul play Informing the referee, just before kick-off, that one of your players is his bank manager.

Freezing Temperature on the particular afternoon at Aberdeen or Invercargill when you've forgotten your gloves and overcoat.

French rugby A term which has come to describe anything which is undisciplined, volatile but somehow successful.

Frustration A team looking around throughout half-time for a dry spot on the ground where they can sit.

Haka The dance the All Blacks perform before eating.

Halfback *See* Scrumhalf.

Halftime To allow spectators to visit the loo, or get another drink, or both.

Headgear Protective bonnet worn to prevent further hair from (1) falling out, or (2) being pulled out.

Heaven Boasts a wonderfully strong rugby team, although a little light on front row forwards and referees.

Heavies One of several names by which these people are known. Also called alicka-doos, pests, necessary evils and officials. They stand at bars, drink Scotch and talk incessantly of how the standard of rugby was ever so much better when they played. They materialise from nowhere at after-match functions and dominate all the speeches. Something current players aspire NOT to be after they retire.

Hip flask Necessary part of rugby watcher's equipment on a brisk winter's afternoon, as well as scarf, programme, mittens, sandwiches, loud-hailer and wife. The last item is optional.

Hooker A sweaty, beastly little fellow, nevertheless having deep religious convictions about the game. Who else raises his arms to the heavens each time he's about to become involved, before dropping devotedly to his knees?

Horrible The feeling you get when you find yourself packing into the front row against an opponent named Luigi and you realise he has eaten heaps of garlic for lunch.

Hurt You are lying wounded on the ground and the coach leans down and says, "It doesn't hurt really . . . " But your ankle is possibly broken and you would much prefer your mum's face than his looking down at you. The fact that you are the goalkicker and the team has just been awarded a penalty with the score at 3–all and only seconds to go has nothing at all to do with his casual dismissal of your injury.

Hush The loud silence which occurs when (1) the ball has left the goalkicker's boot and is heading for the goalposts with the score 16–all and time running out, or (2) the president announces that the club has again incurred a substantial loss for the year, the star first-five has left them for another club and he has been re-elected for his 18th successive year in office.

Hyphen When committeemen find it hard dispensing with their mother's maiden name.

Injury The alternative to having a rest during a game.

Intemperate The scene at 3.00am when you've won the grand final.

HAKA

Intercept Other than pinching the bottom of the president's wife or allowing your son to play soccer, this is considered the most unsporting thing a rugby player can do. Only those in the threequarter line are ever guilty of it which tends to make forwards think of themselves as having higher principles. Just when everthing's going nicely and everyone's having a good time, one rotten sod will slip between two opposing players, catch the ball and run like blazes in the other direction.

J

Jerseys Dairy cows used to keeping the grass down on the playing field, where jersey-pulling takes place.

Jock (1) A Scot who supports the game. (2) Another great supporter of the game. Keeps close contact with the most important parts of rugby and every player would be left hanging loose without one.

Jones Plays hooker for Wales. Also lock, flanker, halfback and on the wing.
See Williams.

Judiciary The naughty lads wind up before members of the judiciary, who have usually failed to be elected to the club committee and thought this the next best thing. They listen to the fictitious ramblings of the culprit who has been sent from the field and then decide what to do with him. Sentences have included dancing with the president's wife at the next social.

K

Kicker A fellow with a certain knack of propulsion who can neutralise the efforts of 15 other players.

Kick-off The reason for the after-match festivities starts here. Constant moves to have this and the following 80 minutes dispensed with altogether have proved unsuccessful, as referees complain that they would feel unwanted.

Knock-on The law states that a knock-on occurs after a player loses possession of the ball, or a player propels or strikes it with his hand or arm, or it strikes a player's hand or arm and then travels forward. Actually, it's unjust discrimination against players with poor eyesight.

L

Lace One of them inevitably breaks just as you're tying up your boots before the most important match of the season. You never have a spare.

Lansdowne Road In Dublin. Not a place for cars but where rugby players run over each other.

Law book Something every spectator knows by heart and no referee has ever read.

League A measure of length varying in different countries, the English land league being three statute miles and the nautical league nearly three and a half. Therefore, rugby players can't understand why they must (1) do extra laps of the oval, (2) have a mouth gargle, or (3) report to the club secretary, if ever they mention the word.

Library Every player worth his salt should have assembled a large collection of rugby books by the time he ascends into the great pitch in the sky. They will range through topics like *How to Pass Your University Exams while Still Playing Rugby*, by Rodney Johnson MA (Hons) and *Unravelling the Mind of a Referee*, Volume II, by Professor Jeremy Smythe-Thompson, to more mundane subjects like *Lions Eaten by Springboks* (a comprehensive analysis of their most recent tour, full stats, vividly illustrated) by JG McK Dobson, of the *Cardiff Bugle*.

Lineout A means of determining who is the best high jumper in each team while being held down, elbowed or bumped. Very difficult, especially as another player has to throw the ball hard at your left armpit at the same time.

Lions When England, Ireland, Scotland and Wales want to make a tour at the same time they solve the problem simply by putting the names of all their international players in a hat, drawing out 30 names and sending them away as one team. Sometimes they play as bravely as lions, so they are called Lions. Other times they don't and Fleet Street calls them lots of other names.

Loosehead First identified in South Africa. A condition afflicting those who play in the front row of the scrum and have one free arm. Only known cure is tightening, in which case the forward concerned becomes known as a tighthead.

Meeting, Annual General Once a year all the officials and players get together. The manager of the third XV grumbles about the number of jerseys that keep getting pinched, the treasurer announces once more that the club is bankrupt, a complaint is heard about the brand of tea being used by the tea ladies and the president is re-elected unopposed once again.

Miss The friendly cry of encouragement to the opposing team's goalkicker as he moves in for a kick at goal.

Mound Small pile of earth upon which kicker places the ball before attempting a goal or kick-off. He must be careful of (1) the ball toppling off the mound just as he is about to make contact, (2) the worm which crawls out from within mound and on to the ball, or (3) green shoots appearing if he takes too long.

Mouthguard An uncomfortable piece of equipment, similar to a baby's dummy which a player only learns about after losing several teeth.

Mud Necessary for at least one game each winter.

Murrayfield Murray used to be an undistinguished forward in the lower grades with Brothers club in Brisbane. Other than the fact he once downed a pint of beer in 11.2 seconds there seems hardly any reason to mention him here. However, he says he has a cousin of the same name who has something important to do with Scottish rugby.

N

M

Maul A scrum or ruck where you are allowed to hold the ball in your hands which leads you to being mauled.

North Island Half of what was left when New Zealand snapped in two. Largely a rural community, producing lambs for slaughter and rugby teams whose opponents share their feeling.

Nose The apparent target of every opposing boot and elbow.

PINETREE

Off side The aroma from the opposite side of the scrum on a particularly hot afternoon.

Oranges Quarters of these are eaten between halves. Old forwards eat the equivalent of an orchard during their career. Coaches have been known to inject them with vodka to (1) make them more tasty, or (2) take the players' minds off the opposing team's 30-point lead.

Ordered off Only necessary when the hot water in the dressing sheds needs switching on before the game ends. The referee usually dispatches a forward on the errand and they never seem to go willingly.

Orthopaedic surgeon The first people an old rugby forward tells when he decides to retire are his orthopaedic surgeon, the club secretary and his wife, in that order.

Parents They run hysterically up and down the touchline at junior rugby matches behaving as they would not otherwise behave. Nevertheless they are necessary for the game's development.

Pass Mostly thrown to good looking birds after the game.

Patches Worn on the jacket elbows to prevent beer on the clubroom bar from soaking through.

Penalty try The only way of scoring a try when you haven't actually earned one. This is where rugby enters the world of supernatural, for the referee has to gaze into his crystal ball and imagine what might have occurred had the player not had his progress interfered with. If you are a referee it's best not to award them. They cause trouble and only mean you'll get pelted with eggs and tomatoes when leaving the field. When a penalty try appears to be "on", you should quickly look away.

Physiotherapist Person with whom a rugby wife is certain her husband is having an affair.

Pinetree Large carnivorous beast which once inhabited the North Island of New Zealand. Ate opposing forwards without so much as chewing them. Avoided capture for many years but finally slowed down with age, allowing anthropologists to approach close enough to identify and name it. Was tagged Colinptus Earlingus Meads, or Pinetree for short.

Pontypool Patch of land in Wales where they grow rugby nuts by sprinkling them with coal dust.

Pot (1) As an "Another pot, guv'nor and don't take all day, the coach'll be back soon." (2) When the first-five seeks to "have a pot" by kicking the ball between the posts after first dropping it to the ground. He usually misses.

President Constantly makes reference in his speeches to his playing days which nobody but himself seems to recall. Drinks Scotch and shakes hands with equal enthusiasm. Has been questioned by more than one player about his parentage and told that the club would get on a damned sight better without him. He ignores such talk.

Prop Short support, hewn from timber or similar dense matter, upon which the hooker leans.

Pumas Cougars or mountain lions. Also the name of Argentina's national team and like their namesakes prove troublesome at times.

Punt The action of one of the threequarters when all else fails. He hoofs the ball high in the air hoping it will (1) land on an opponent's head and knock him senseless, or (2) bounce favourably so that he can chase and catch it, thus making a big name for himself. Usually the opposition gets it and simply returns it by the same method.

Query When the skipper momentarily loses his senses and asks the referee why he penalised Tom Pudding for being off side, when in fact he was lying in an off side position but was at the same time being treated for a broken leg.

Questionable Referees sometimes make these decisions. Everybody thinks they're wrong but aren't game to say so.

Quick Your description of the opposing player who has just comprehensively beaten you on the outside and scored the match winning try under the goalposts. *See* Genius.

Records Rugby journals, books and magazines are full of all sorts of uninteresting statistical information about highest scores, lowest scores, number of goals kicked, successive wins, longest-serving presidents, fattest forwards and so forth. But many other pieces of information, far more interesting than these, go largely unrecorded, such as the *Most Unsporting Gesture*: To avoid sharing the ball with the opposition, forwards from the New South Wales Country team stuck the ball up the jersey of one of their kind while playing archrivals Sydney in 1975. The game continued for some minutes before the absence was noted. Country won 22–20.

Referee Was given a whistle as a small boy and enjoys blowing it constantly. Interrupts what would otherwise be an exciting stoppage-free game of rugby. Can recite Law 26 (3) (f) quicker than the date of his wife's birthday. Has no colour sense, sticking mostly to white co-ordinates. Has a very divisive effect on the game as half the people love him (the winners) and the other half think he's (1) blind, (2) a rotten cheat, or (3) both.

Replacement The cleanest looking player on the field at the end of the match.

Reserves' bench A panel of dejected souls.

Retirement Must occur sooner or later but it's remarkable how many times it takes place just as the youngster in the team below starts to impress the selectors.

Ruck A disorganised scrum, where the forwards and referee are not entirely sure what's happening and in which the ball generally gets mislaid.

Rugby A pastime of delirious enjoyment, much story-telling, plentiful drinking and occasional singing disturbed only by 80 minutes of often pointless endeavour on a strip of barren earth.

Rugger The only persons allowed to use this as an alternative word for rugby are those in direct succession to the throne, or those who think they might be.

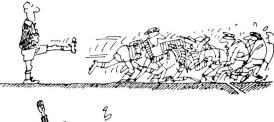

REFEREE

Scarf	Common piece of apparel, knitted in the club colours and used to identify those people who are not playing.
Scissors	(1) A movement where players criss-cross in order to confuse the opposition. (2) The instrument used to untangle knotted bootlaces after the game.
Scoreboard	The infernal apparatus at the edge of the ground which constantly reminds you just how many points you are behind.
Scrumhalf	Not eight players (which is half the scrum) but the little fellow called half (who is not half a man but a full-grown man known as half) who feeds the scrum (which is 16 men). Like his name, he causes confusion.
Scrum machine	An inert object.
Scrummage	A rather complex arrangement of arms and legs. In fact the only reason for its existence is so that the opposing front rowers can exchange jokes. Sometimes, if they can't agree who's going to tell the first story, they fight.
Selectors	Men with pins who pick teams.

Sevens, or seven-a-side	If the opposition doesn't turn up, you divide your team in half, make the one left over the ref and play sevens or seven-a-side. And if half your team doesn't turn up, you can divide what's left in half, make one the ref and play threes or three-a-side.
Shorts	In which a rugby player spends many happy hours trying to get dirty and his poor mum many unhappy hours trying to get clean. Manufactured with care so that at least one pair rips during every international match.
Shove	The forward momentum used in scrummaging and crowded bars.
Singing	An integral part of rugby, ranging from the soothing lullaby of a mother singing to her infant in an effort to drown the noise of the rugby international father is watching on television, to the thunderous sounds of 60,000 Welshmen clearing their throats at the same international.
Sir	The name players call a referee to his face, as in "Please sir, is that law in the book or did you just make it up?" Behind his back they call him other names.
Skin	Donations of this are made by rugby players to all groundsmen, who consider it excellent fertiliser.
Springbok	A species of antelope in danger of extinction.
South Island	The other half of New Zealand. *See* North Island.
Stab kick	A kick (1) keeping low to the ground with the purpose of going beyond the attacking line, or (2) as in stab-in-the-dark. Even the kicker doesn't know where it's headed.
Stitches	The state the captain lapses into when you announce that you're sick and tired of playing front row and forthwith want to be considered for the wing.
Studs	The reasons for their use have never been fully documented. (1) They are generally thought to have been placed on the underside of players' boots to make it easier to avoid the chewing gum on dressing room floors. (2) Obviously of great assistance to groundsmen, as they furrow the soil ready for the seeding of next summer's cricket pitch. Also, mother's immediate thought when told by daughter that she is going to a party given by the local rugby team.

Suggestions They are always being generously passed on to the referee, as in, "Hey ref, why don't ya get ya bleedin' eyes tested . . . ?"

Summer That time of the year when kids recognise their rugby-playing father more readily. The lawn gets mowed, the back fence fixed and the lounge room painted.

Sunday morning You wake and wish you had not consumed that last pint of beer the night before. Of course your state of health has nothing to do with the 17 or 18 pints before that. Your head and body ache in unison and you wish Sundays could be eliminated from the week.

Tackle A part of the game in which you have no particular interest. It involves trying to provide an obstacle for an opponent to fall over.

Team lists Those strips of paper displayed before each match showing who is playing in which team. Only the bravest start by looking at the first XV. The quickest ways of locating your name is to start with the Extra A 111s and work upwards.

Team talk (1) Delaying tactics by the coach to stop his players getting to the pub before closing time. (2) The alternative to training if it's too cold outside. (3) When the coach tries to explain what he wanted done in the last match and why it wasn't. (4) When the president calls the players together to inform them that the local publican has complained about their behaviour and moves a motion that they shift to another pub.

Thought Behind every excuse in rugby. The winger says "Gosh skipper, I thought he was going to run straight ahead instead of using footwork like Fred Astaire and finishing up behind me . . .". Or the drawling prop who has just conceded a penalty at 12–all with only minutes left says, "I'm sorry fellas but I haven't touched a footy for a coupla years and thought nobody would mind if I touched it in the scrum just this once . . ."

Throw in You throw your wallet, car keys and false teeth into a bag held by the team manager for safe keeping and hope you get all or some of them back after the game.

Ties Necessary piece of clothing, although nobody ever seems to buy them, only give them away. Committeemen are particularly fond of them, as they cover the naked midriff where the bottom shirt button parts from the small aperture in which it is supposed to be inserted.

Tighthead The result of a loosehead being tightened.

Timekeeper The man who waits until the visiting team is only one point behind and busily pressing your goalline before deciding to ring the fulltime bell.

Toast (1) Anyone or anything used as a reason to start the drinking at rugby dinners, or (2) when the opposition are 30 points ahead they are said to have you "on toast".

Touch A line separating the players from the spectators. Kickers hardly ever find it when they want to and too often find it when they don't.

Touch-in-goal When your team mate snips you for a fiver while you're waiting in the in-goal area for a kick to be taken.

Trainer A contemporary slave-driver whose task is to get teams at least remotely fit for the beginning of the season. Relishes pain and suffering. Players retaliate by deflating their car tyres and hiding his whip.

Training When your team practises all the secret moves it never gets to use during a match.

Trophies Are indispensible to the game of rugby and awarded at the end of each season to various deserving people, including the club member who spent most money at the bar, the player who attended most training sessions and the girlfriend or wife who didn't miss a match. The fact she cannot remember a single score doesn't count.

Try There are two kinds of tries (1) What your dear old mum tells you to do as you walk out the garden gate, "Try not to get your shorts too dirty, Billy . . . ' and (2) what your coach says to you in the dressing room, "Try your bleedin' 'arts out there today lads . . . and don't come back if ya lose."

Tweed A twilled woollen cloth which rugby players use in their jackets to identify themselves from non-rugby types.

Twickenham (Twickers) Famous UK habitat of birds, either streaking, or being consumed with champers in the carpark.

U

Ughhh The escaping sound as opposing front rows thump down against one another in the scrum. Also their dialogue together after the game.

University That team whose shorts are a little longer, socks a little higher and birds better looking.

Unkind Words the coach uses to you in the dressing room when the game's over. You plead that you couldn't help it if the opposing winger crossed for six tries. The sun was in your eyes.

Unwise The decision to remain on the ground near the ball when the All Blacks decide it is theirs for the taking. Stone monuments have been erected to this sort of hero.

Up-and-under If you're a spectator and it starts raining, commonsense tells you to get up and under shelter. An up-and-under on the field is the same as a Garryowen. It's best to get clear of them, too.

Upright The first-five who calls the ref's attention to the fact that the pass he has just thrown was slightly forward.

Utility player Not much good in any position.

TROPHIES

Valleys More commonly known as The Valleys. An area of South Wales smeared with coal dust where men from towns and villages with odd sounding names drink beer, work, sing and play rugby in equal proportions.

Vice-captain In charge of the team's activities after dark.

Victory A player realises it has happened only when he finds the dressing shed more crowded than when he left it.

Wales They have never been beaten at rugby, although other teams have been known to score more points.

Wallabies Smallish kangaroos which spend their life jumping all over the place. Despite their size, big men in black and even lions have occasionally been frightened by them.

Water (1) Magic liquid rubbed on to injuries during a game which instantly cures broken limbs, bleeding noses and bruised joints. (2) What the club president uses sparingly in his Scotch.

Weak The feeling when you're about to pack into the first scrum of the game against a rival prop twice your size, who possesses no teeth, has a nose bent like an elbow and constantly makes threatening noises. Your other prop steadfastly refuses to change positions with you, adding, "Any last words for the family . . . ?"

Whistle The most persecuted implement in rugby, as the referee is always being told to (1) throw it away, (2) swallow it, or (3) put it in a most uncomfortable place.

Williams Plays for Wales where Jones doesn't. *See* Jones.

William Webb Ellis Had it not been for young Billy's impetuosity, lawns would be tended, dogs washed, sinks unclogged, gardens weeded and rooms painted on Saturday afternoons. A tablet set in the wall surrounding the playing fields at Rugby School perpetuates his memory in the following terms: "This stone commemorates the exploits of WW Ellis who, with a fine disregard for the rules of football as played in his time, first took the ball in his arms and ran with it thus originating the distinctive feature of the rugby game. AD 1823." William Webb Ellis subsequently entered the church and became the incumbent at St Clement's Dane in The Strand in London but there is no record of him ever retaining an active interest in the game he so inspiringly founded. Just think what he missed.

Wind Can be quite distracting at times in rucks, mauls and scrums.

Wingers Speedy players who run away from the hard stuff and into the scoreline.

Wisdom Dating the ugly daughter of the chairman of selectors.

Wives Are extremely grateful to William Webb Ellis for inventing a way of allowing them to knit for at least 80 minutes without being disturbed.

Women's rugby Started in the United States (which you might have expected). Now growing there in popularity. The wives and girlfriends of players thought that if you can't beat 'em then join 'em. The husband or boyfriend who wore old pantyhose under his shorts to prevent grazing now has to buy his own.

Writers Sometimes they are celebrated old players with arthritic knees but mostly they were hidden away on the wing of their school's third XV. They delight in telling current players how they ought to play the game.

X-ray The favourite pastime of club doctors is sending players off to hospital for x-rays. They have been known to elope with pretty radiographers.

Y

Yaaamuuug Quaint Down Under expression to suggest that the referee should perhaps be better informed on the laws of the game.

Yanks Have taken to rugby like politicians to a microphone. Early problems caused by Texans wanting to wear their 10-gallon hats, six-shooters and spurs during a game and the Red Indians in the team wanting to take scalps if they won have now almost been abolished.

Z

Zero Your team's score when you haven't done very well.

Zzzzzzzzzzz Sounds emanating from outside the fence when the referee is trying to demonstrate to the players just how much he knows about the laws.

WINGERS

The Rugby Dictionary was published in Australia by Sun Books, Melbourne, in 1985.
Its author Jim Webster was for a long time a prominent sports writer on the *Sydney Morning Herald* and reported on many Wallaby tours. In 1990 he wrote Simon Poidevin's biography.   Cartoons by : PAT MALLET

PROFILE : VILIAMI OFAHENGAUE

Full name: Viliami Ofahengaue.

Birthdate: May 3, 1968.

Zodiac sign: Taurus.

Birthplace: Tonga.

Residence: Sydney, Australia.

Occupation: Piling contractor.

Height: 1.93m.

Weight: 100kg.

Marital status: Single.

Position: Breakaway or No 8.

Present club: Manly.

Previous club: Seddon High School, Auckland.

Most difficult opponent: Paul Henderson.

Best rugby memory: Playing first game against an international team, Sydney versus France.

Biggest disappointment: Being kicked out of New Zealand.

Favourite country: Tonga.

Biggest influence on career: My father.

Other sports/leisure interests: Volley ball, touch football, sleeping.

Favourite rugby ground: Sydney Sports Stadium.

Favourite film: *Coming to America.*

Favourite TV show: *Candid Camera.*

Favourite music: UB40.

Favourite food: Pig and more pig.

Funniest rugby experience: Losing my pants in the first test at Christchurch.

Biggest drag in rugby: Training.

PROFILE : WILL CARLING

Full name: William David Charles Carling.

Birthdate: December 12, 1965.

Zodiac sign: Sagittarius.

Birthplace: Bradford-On-Avon, Wiltshire.

Residence: London.

Occupation: Trainee oil executive.

Height: 1.8m.

Weight: 87kg.

Years playing rugby: 11.

Position: Centre.

Present club: Harlequins.

International experience: England since January, 1988.

Most difficult opponent: Philippe Sella (France).

Best rugby memory: Beating Australia, 1988.

Most memorable match: England versus Australia, 1988.

Biggest disappointments: Not making first World Cup; missing 1989 Lions tour of Australia through injury; losing to Scotland in 1990 Five Nations championship.

Favourite country: Ireland.

Biggest influence on career: My father.

Other sports/leisure interests: Squash, golf, cricket, painting.

Favourite rugby grounds: Twickenham; school ground.

Favourite film: *Animal House.*

Favourite TV shows: *Only Fools and Horses*; *Fawlty Towers.*

Favourite music: Tina Turner, Paul McCartney, Rubert Palmer.

Favourite food: Chicken.

Funniest rugby experience: Going on tour with Paul Rendall.

B4

B5

FOCUS ON
1991 RUGBY WORLD CUP

By BARRY NEWCOMBE

The juggernaut World Cup approaches. Compared with the pioneer event in New Zealand and Australia in 1987, the 1991 competition based in England, Ireland, Scotland, Wales and France, with a final at Twickenham, home of the game, on November 2, is mammoth.

It will generate vastly more money, bigger crowds, more television and radio time and more newspaper space, and make greater demands on the fitness and staying power of players than even the veterans of '87 might have predicted.

It is astonishing that in the five years since the initial launch plans for the World Cup were announced country after country has had to completely rethink its attitude to international football.

In the Five Nations' championship, which has created pride and history for its competitors and envy from others, there is now the thought that it is only a high pressure build-up for the World Cup.

The championship is tough to win but it is now nothing like the prize of beating the rest of the world.

What did 1990 sort out in terms of form? New Zealand's first defeat since 1986 came at exactly the right time in my view because it gave the All Blacks time to rethink their priorities before the tour to France and it did not seriously weaken their place as favourites to retain the Cup.

It is true that the All Blacks do not dominate as they once did. But what other nation could suffer the losses to rugby league and still cling on?

What other nation could lose players of the calibre of Michael Jones and Wayne Shelford from their back row and still cling on?

That ability to cling on will stand the All Blacks in good stead. After all, they still have the components of an excellent team because of Grant Fox, because of the front row, because of Gary Whetton, and because the New Zealand system is better geared to producing quality and durability than any other competing nation.

England looked ready to set the world alight when it stormed through the first three matches in the 1990 championship against Ireland, France and Wales.

But in the Grand Slam decider against Scotland at Murrayfield, England came badly unstuck, raising doubts about its abilities to play under pressure. Perhaps England can only lead from the front and has no concept of turning a game.

On top of the defeat to Scotland, England took a below strength team to Argentina for an out-of-context seven match tour in July and lost the second test — the first time it had fallen to any nation outside the original International Board line-up.

So England started the run-in to the World Cup full of doubts. On top of that there were plenty of players in the other home countries who believed that the England side would be ageing fast by World Cup time . . . and that the next players in line would not be up to it.

Scotland, lifted to new heights by taking the Grand Slam, learned still more on its New Zealand tour and was not disgraced in the two tests.

It might not fare so well in the 1991 championship because it has to play France and England away. But it has plenty of confidence in the bank.

Wales went to Namibia and scrambled some victories together which were needed after its first championship whitewash in history.

It has had a terrible 10 years and coach Ron Waldron and his advisers have to hope they can produce a short term salvage job in '91 before the effects of the new Welsh leagues begin to be felt.

Ireland was the only home country not to tour in 1990. Like Wales it is short on confidence and new coach Ciaran Fitzgerald has a considerable task on his hands to try to make it a better Cup side in the second competition than it was in the first.

France remains the mystery team. Since finishing runner-up to the All Blacks in the 1987 Cup final in Auckland, France has drifted away from its cherished position of the best side in Europe.

It has been through troubled times and the head of coach Jacques Fouroux has been on the line so often that it is remarkable he has survived. But he might still be able to conjure up a Cup challenge because the whole business simply suits the French mood.

Waiting for the World Cup to become reality in Europe has been accompanied by positive reports from all venues.

World Cup fever such as we experienced in New Zealand in 1987 is certain to be repeated, beginning with the opening match between England and New Zealand at Twickenham.

Twickenham has a new north stand, seating 16,000, to host England's group matches and the final itself. But all the major grounds of the Five Nations, and a few lesser ones, will burst with World Cup emotions.

The key matches in the groups are England versus New Zealand, Scotland versus Ireland, Wales versus Australia and France versus Fiji. These are the eight seeded nations and the results from their matches should determine the quarter-final line-up.

But what are the possibilities of upsets? Could Argentina or Western Samoa cause problems for Wales or Australia? Western Samoa comes from a hard school and there is no telling what day after day of training for the Cup will do for its competitive instincts. Argentina has a rugby heritage which cannot be denied.

The United States and Canada will know the value of a victory over one of the big nations and similarly Romania could be out to make an impact now that rugby has become re-established as a leading sport in the country.

Of the top eight countries no team is more fortunate than Scotland.

It is co-hosting a group with Ireland and toss of the coin means that Scotland will play the Irish at Murrayfield and will continue to play at home in the quarter-final and semi-final stage if it keeps winning — a thrilling prospect for David Sole and his men.

The World Cup will put modern rugby on trial to its biggest ever global audience. In England alone it will be the biggest sporting event since the 1966 world soccer cup and the games and the players will be scrutinised, analysed and glorified as never before.

But I believe that the essential core spirit of rugby will remain much the same as it was in the 1987 Cup. Some players will be involved for a second time, lending their experience to their squads. Others will be new, learning minute by minute.

The matches they play will be at the sharp end of the Cup but I am sure that the welcome given to the competing nations, all the way from the south of France to the south of Scotland, will put a mark on the players of 1991 which will never be removed. ∎

1991 WORLD CUP TOURNAMENT SCHEDULE

Thursday, October 3	England v New Zealand	Twickenham
Friday, October 4	Australia v Argentina	Llanelli
	France v Romania	Beziers
Saturday, October 5	Italy v USA	Otley
	Scotland v Japan	Murrayfield
	Fiji v Canada	Bayonne
Sunday, October 6	Wales v Western Samoa	Cardiff Arms Park
	Ireland v Zimbabwe	Dublin
Tuesday, October 8	New Zealand v USA	Gloucester
	England v Italy	Twickenham
	France v Fiji	Grenoble
Wednesday, October 9	Wales v Argentina	Cardiff Arms Park
	Scotland v Zimbabwe	Murrayfield
	Ireland v Japan	Dublin
	Australia v Western Samoa	Pontypool
	Canada v Romania	Grenoble
Friday, October 11	England v USA	Twickenham
Saturday, October 12	Scotland v Ireland	Murrayfield
	Wales v Australia	Cardiff Arms Park
	France v Canada	Agen
Sunday, October 13	New Zealand v Italy	Leicester
	Fiji v Romania	Brive
Monday, October 14	Zimbabwe v Japan	Belfast
	Argentina v Western Samoa	Pontypridd
Saturday, October 19	Winner Pool 2 v runner-up Pool 3	Murrayfield
	Winner Pool 4 v runner-up Pool 1	Parc des Princes
Sunday, October 20	Winner Pool 3 v runner-up Pool 2	Lansdowne Road
	Winner Pool 1 v runner-up Pool 4	Lille
Saturday, October 26	B v C : Semi-final	Murrayfield
Sunday, October 27	A v D : Semi-final	Lansdowne Road
Wednesday, October 30	The Play-off	Cardiff Arms Park
Saturday, November 2	The Final	Twickenham

Barry Newcombe is the rugby correspondent of the *Sunday Express* in London.
He is also the internationally recognised tennis correspondent for the same publication and has reported on most grand slam tennis tournaments and major international rugby events over the past decade.

1991 RUGBY WORLD CUP

EUROPEAN ZONE

Czechoslovakia
Yugoslavia
Portugal
West Germany
Netherlands
Sweden
Denmark
Switzerland
Israel

Netherlands

Sweden

Spain
Belgium
Netherlands
Poland

Italy
Spain
Netherlands
Romania

Italy
winner to Pool 1
Romania
runner-up to Pool 4

AFRICAN ZONE

Ivory Coast
Morocco
Tunisia
Zimbabwe

Zimbabwe
winner to Pool 2

ASIAN/PACIFIC ZONE

Malaysia
Hong Kong
Taiwan
Sri Lanka
Korea

Japan
Tonga
Korea
Western Samoa

Western Samoa
winner to Pool 3
Japan
runner-up to Pool 2

AMERICAN ZONE

United States
Argentina
Canada

Canada
winner to Pool 4
Argentina
runner-up to Pool 3
United States
third to Pool 1

THE DRAW (seeded teams in capitals)

Pool 1 (in England)
NEW ZEALAND
ENGLAND
Italy
United States

Pool 2 (in Wales)
AUSTRALIA
WALES
Western Samoa
Argentina

Pool 3 (in Scotland)
SCOTLAND
IRELAND
Zimbabwe
Japan

Pool 4 (in France)
FRANCE
FIJI
Canada
Romania

QUARTER-FINALS

1. Winner Pool 1 versus runner-up Pool 4, in France
2. Winner Pool 4 versus runner-up Pool 1, in France
3. Winner Pool 2 versus runner-up Pool 3, in Edinburgh
4. Winner Pool 3 versus runner-up Pool 2, in Dublin

SEMI-FINALS

1. Winner 1 versus winner 4, in Dublin
2. Winner 2 versus winner 3, in Edinburgh

THIRD PLACE PLAY-OFF

in Cardiff

FINAL : NOVEMBER 2

at Twickenham

THE FIRST WORLD CUP, 1987 – HOW THE NATIONS FARED

POOL ONE	Australia	England	Japan	United States
Australia		19–6	42–23	47–12
England	6–19		60–7	34–6
Japan	23–42	7–60		18–21
United States	12–47	6–34	21–18	

Standings: 1 Australia, 2 England, 3 United States, 4 Japan.

POOL TWO	Canada	Ireland	Tonga	Wales
Canada		19–46	37–4	9–40
Ireland	46–19		32–9	6–13
Tonga	4–37	9–32		16–29
Wales	40–9	13–6	29–16	

Standings: 1 Wales, 2 Ireland, 3 Canada, 4 Tonga.

POOL THREE	Argentina	Fiji	Italy	New Zealand
Argentina		9–28	25–16	15–46
Fiji	28–9		15–18	13–74
Italy	16–25	18–15		6–70
New Zealand	46–15	74–13	70–6	

Standings: 1 New Zealand, 2 Fiji, 3 Italy, 4 Argentina. (Fiji scored 6 tries, Italy 5 and Argentina 4, which separated the teams after finishing with a win each.)

POOL FOUR	France	Romania	Scotland	Zimbabwe
France		55–12	20–20	70–12
Romania	12–55		28–55	21–20
Scotland	20–20	55–28		60–21
Zimbabwe	12–70	20–21	21–60	

Standings: 1 France, 2 Scotland, 3 Romania, 4 Zimbabwe.
(France qualified ahead of Scotland because it scored 3 tries to Scotland's 2 in their encounter.)

THE FIRST WORLD CUP, 1987 – HOW THE NATIONS FARED

QUARTER-FINALS

New Zealand 30, Scotland 3 at Christchurch
France 31, Fiji 16 at Auckland
Australia 33, Ireland 15 at Sydney
Wales 16, England 3 at Brisbane

SEMI-FINALS

France 30, Australia 24 at Sydney
New Zealand 49, Wales 6 at Brisbane

PLAY-OFF FOR THIRD

Wales 22, Australia 21 at Rotorua

GRAND FINAL

New Zealand 29, France 9 at Auckland

GRAND FINAL DETAILS

NEW ZEALAND

John Gallagher; Craig Green, Joe Stanley, John Kirwan (try); Warwick Taylor, Grant Fox (con, 4 pens, pot); David Kirk (capt); Wayne Shelford; Michael Jones (try), Gary Whetton, Murray Pierce, Alan Whetton; Steve McDowell, Sean Fitzpatrick, John Drake.

FRANCE

Serge Blanco; Didier Camberabero (con, pen), Philippe Sella, Patrice Lagisquet; Denis Charvet, Franck Mesnel; Pierre Berbizier (try); Laurent Rodriguez; Eric Champ, Jean Condom, Alain Lorieux, Dominique Erbani; Pascal Ondarts, Daniel Dubroca (capt), Jean-Pierre Garuet.

Referee : Kerry Fitzgerald (Australia)
Crowd : 46,000

FIVE who shared in the World Cup victory celebrations in 1987 even though they weren't required to strip for the final against France — from left, Kieran Crowley, Andy Earl, Mark Brooke-Cowden, Terry Wright and Albert Anderson.

Photo by : PETER BUSH

PICTORIAL HIGHLIGHTS OF THE FIRST WORLD CUP, 1987

TOP: David Kirk, who led the side and Andy Dalton, the unlucky captain who sat out the entire campaign injured, show their delight with the All Blacks' 29–9 grand final victory against France at Eden Park. ABOVE: Kirk and his mighty team line out at Ballymore for the national anthems before the semi-final clash against Wales.

Photos by : PETER BUSH

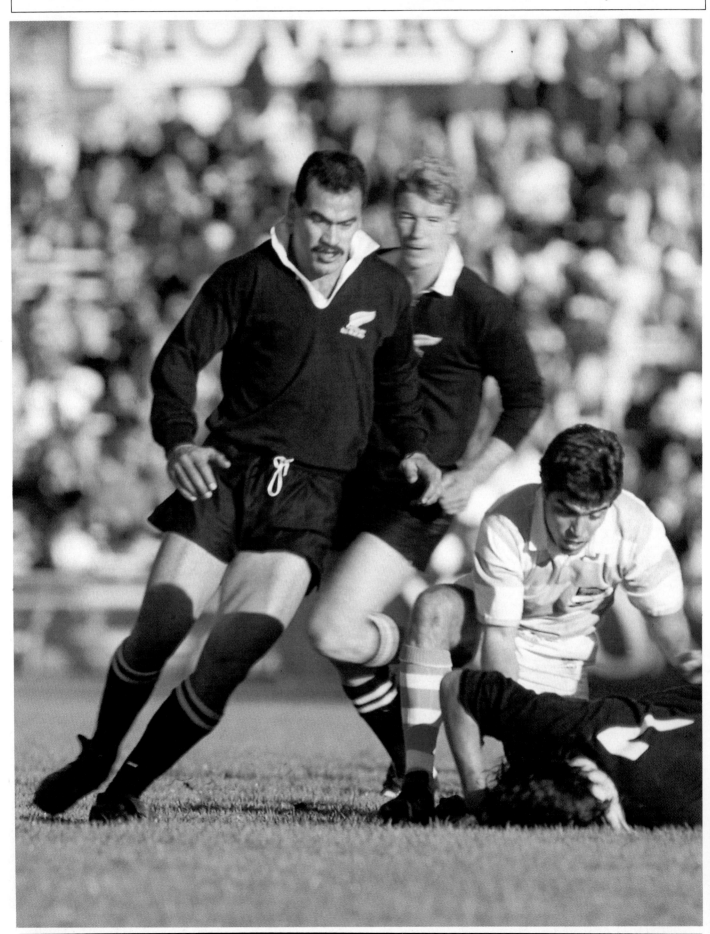

JOE STANLEY and John Kirwan target the action during New Zealand's pool match with Argentina at Athletic Park. The All Blacks won 46–15.

Photo by : PETER BUSH

PICTORIAL HIGHLIGHTS OF THE FIRST WORLD CUP, 1987

TOP: Who said the Welsh always play in scarlet jerseys? For their pool match with Tonga at Palmerston North in 1987 the Welsh donned green jerseys and came out on top. Wales went through to claim third placing in the first World Cup. ABOVE LEFT: Part of the fanfare that marked the opening of the first World Cup. ABOVE RIGHT: Wales and Ireland contest lineout ball during their windswept pool match at Athletic Park. Wales won 13–6.

Photos by : PETER BUSH

1991 WORLD CUP

ARGENTINA

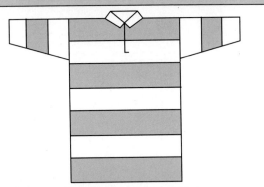

JAPAN

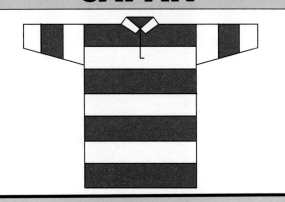

CANADA

ROMANIA

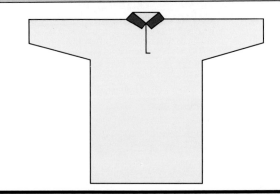

FIJI

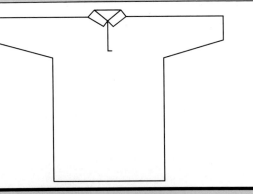

UNITED STATES

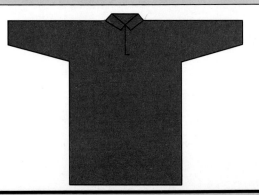

IRELAND

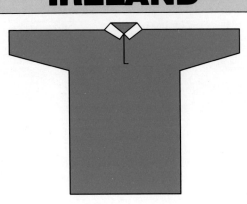

WESTERN SAMOA

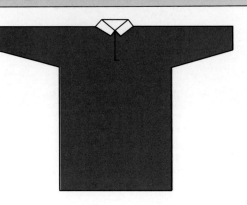

THE QUALIFIERS

AUSTRALIA

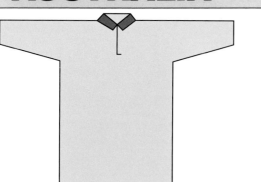

NEW ZEALAND

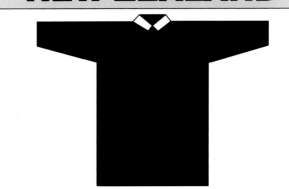

ENGLAND

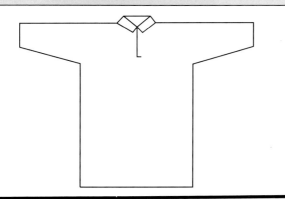

SCOTLAND

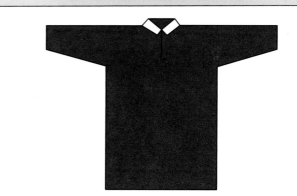

FRANCE

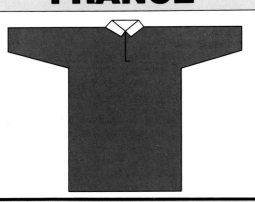

WALES

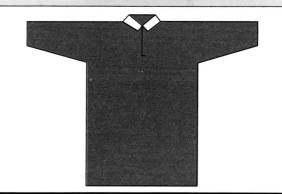

ITALY

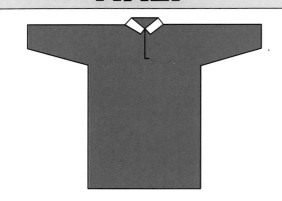

ZIMBABWE

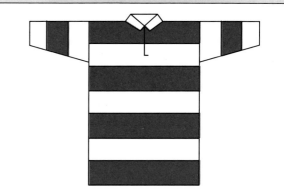

GRANT FOX
– THE BEEN THERE, DONE THAT PLAYER

■ By BOB HOWITT■

GRANT FOX . . . goalkicker extraordinary.

Photo by : PHOTOSPORT

Because he has now shattered just about every pointscoring record available to him and been such a high profile figure for so long, there's a tendency to think Grant Fox has commanded the No 10 jersey since he first aspired to the All Blacks.

But not so. Fox, now 28, had to serve a lengthy apprenticeship and didn't become New Zealand's regular test first-five until the World Cup campaign of 1987.

By the time he got there he knew what it was like to warm the reserves' bench and be bypassed for big matches.

"Been there, done that," admits Foxy, who as an incomparable matchwinner has firmly cemented himself at first-five in the All Black test line-up over the past four seasons.

Because most of the focus on Fox these days is on his phenomenal goalkicking achievements it is probably timely to remind readers that Fox, like most aspiring footballers, had to spend his share of time in the shadow of others.

It was John Hart who introduced Fox to representative rugby, installing him at first-five in his first season coaching Auckland, 1982.

Fox, who'd demonstrated his potential as a New Zealand secondary schools representative in 1980, was only 20 and took a while to find his feet.

The *Rugby Annual* of 1982 notes that Fox "took time to settle into the higher pace of first-class rugby and to adjust to the physical drain of Colts and representative toil".

The next year, the year in which John Kirwan was introduced, Fox made steady if unspectacular progress. His dropped goal allowed Auckland to snatch a late victory over the British Lions but Auckland fizzled horribly at season's end, losing 9–31 to Canterbury in its Ranfurly Shield bid (yes, those were the days when Auckland could still lose a shield game) and 12–25 to Waikato (a notable happening, for Auckland hasn't lost a national championship fixture on Eden Park since).

The *Annual* this time observed that Fox was "an eminently steady goalkick. This was Fox's settling-in season, for he did not run very much and concentrated on moving or kicking the ball. Next year Fox should lift his game a notch, and work on his running".

Well, the next year Fox did just that. Auckland enjoyed stunning success, averaging 46 points a game and running in

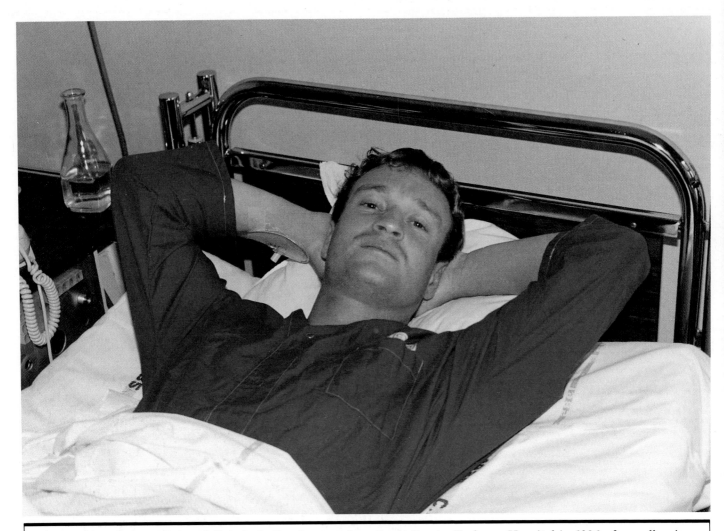

LOOKING comfortable but definitely feeling frustrated — Grant Fox in Toulouse Hospital in 1986 after collapsing during the All Blacks' tour.

Photo by : BOB HOWITT

103 tries. The *Annual* elevated Fox to player of the year and the national selectors were so impressed with him they named him for the All Blacks' short end-of-season tour of Fiji.

Wayne Smith was the test incumbent in 1984 and Fox had to settle for two midweek appearances in Suva — against the President's XV and an Eastern XV.

His debut was at the National Stadium and he marked it with a 19 point performance though in his other outing the first-choice goalkicker was fullback Mark Finlay.

Fox wasn't needed for the two home tests against England in 1985, his next taste of international rugby coming in Argentina in October.

It wasn't supposed to be Argentina. It was supposed to be South Africa, but of course the courts blocked that and so the Pumas, not the Springboks, became the All Blacks' prey.

Fox seemed fated to remain a midweek player until Smith was laid low with a kidney infection and suddenly the Aucklander found himself making his test debut in front of 30,000 boisterous Latins

in Buenos Aires opposite the player many regarded as the finest flyhalf in the world, Hugo Porta.

Fox was unfazed and contributed handsomely to his team's thrilling 33–20 victory. He matched Porta's dropped goal and outdid the maestro with the pinpoint accuracy of his up-and-unders. The goalkicking duties were in the hands of Kieran Crowley.

Smith, restored to health, displaced Fox for the second test which was drawn 21–all. And that brought down the curtain on 1985.

Things became rather murky in 1986, for the Cavaliers decided to bypass all the normal systems — and the courts — and undertake an independent tour of South Africa, which naturally created an uproar.

While people expostulated back home, it was rugby business as normal in South Africa, with the Springboks and the Cavaliers tackling each other in four tests on successive Saturdays.

Fox was preferred ahead of Smith for the first three tests and proceeded to match another of the world's outstanding

first-fives, Naas Botha, certainly in goal-kicking accuracy.

But Fox's boot wasn't enough and the Springboks triumphed three tests to one. Bringing Smith in for the finale at Ellis Park might have added speed to the backline but it didn't save the series.

While he'd been in South Africa a young fellow from North Harbour, Frano Botica, secured the vacant All Black test berth and made such a good fist of it, he survived for the season; indeed, he was named New Zealand player of the year.

Fox supporters expected him to displace Botica in the test line-up when the All Blacks then toured France.

Things didn't work out that way. In fact, they didn't work out at all. Fox appeared in three midweek night fixtures, at Strasbourg, Toulon and Bayonne and spent the last week of the tour in hospital.

Against Cote Basque at Bayonne he was tackled heavily and suffered internal bruising. Fortunately, the tour selectors preferred Botica for the first test at Toulouse because Fox, after watching from the grandstand, collapsed and was rushed to hospital.

A lot of water had to be drained from his lungs, and he remained — rather forlornly — in Toulouse Hospital when his colleagues moved on to Nantes via La Rochelle.

"It was," Fox recalls, "an experience with a difference.

"I was intrigued to find a carafe of wine being served with every meal they brought me. That's the French way."

Communication was difficult because of the language barrier but the hospital staff looked after him well enough until he was recovered sufficiently to rejoin the team in Nantes.

It didn't hasten the mending when the All Blacks were beaten out of sight by the French 16–3.

At that stage not Fox, not anyone immediately associated with the All Blacks, would have predicted the success that would follow.

It would be four years from Nantes (to a murky afternoon at Athletic Park in August, 1990) before the All Blacks would lose again.

In between they would sweep all before them in the World Cup, put 104 points on Japan in Tokyo and complete unbeaten runs through Australia, Wales and Ireland.

It would all start, soon after Fox returned home and while he was still convalescing.

The New Zealand Rugby Union would promote John Hart and Alex Wyllie, the stunningly successful coaches of Auckland and Canterbury, on to the national panel with Brian Lochore, and collectively they would formulate a plan that would take New Zealand clear of the rest of the rugby world.

Throughout what were to become four golden years only one player would wear the test No 10 jersey — Grant Fox.

His stranglehold on the position would see Frano Botica defect to league.

Starting with a haul of 126 points in six World Cup contests, Fox would soon eclipse Don Clarke's test point-scoring record and would break the hearts of many international sides with his unerring boot.

Fox is a perfectionist. He practises regularly, and doesn't slacken after a perfect goalkicking display — of which there

SAY, isn't that . . . ? Yes, it has to be. It's a teenage Grant Fox doing his thing for Auckland Grammar School a decade ago.

have been several outstanding examples.

In fact, he claims he's probably put in more practice in 1990 than ever before which, he confesses, has helped his confidence.

"In 1990, for the first time, I've had no concern with nervousness, even in the most important fixtures.

"I have been completely relaxed when goalkicking — it's been great." ∎

Bob Howitt has been editor of *Rugby News* and the *New Zealand Rugby Annual* since their inceptions 20 years ago. Among New Zealand's most prolific writers he has followed almost every All Black tour since the mid-1960s.

A RUGBY QUIZ
– 100 TOPICAL QUESTIONS
Set by GRANT HARDING

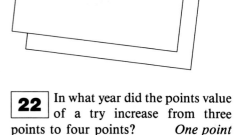

1 The Southland Rugby Union changed the name of its ground in 1989 from Rugby Park to what? *One point*

2 Name the current All Black who held New Zealand titles for Judo. *One point*

3 One of the current All Blacks has a father who was an All Black in the 1950s — name him. *One point*

4 What was the score when Auckland won the Ranfurly Shield off Canterbury in 1985? *One point*

5 Name the current Otago representative who has written children's stories. *One point*

6 Name the respective captains of Counties, Auckland, Otago and Wellington during the 1990 season. *Four points*

7 In what year did Wayne Shelford make his All Black debut? *One point*

8 Who is the New Zealand Rugby Football Union chairman? *One point*

9 Name the former Australian international who played for Ireland against the All Blacks in 1989. *One point*

10 Name the two universities attended by 1987 World Cup captain David Kirk. *Two points*

11 Only four teams held the Ranfurly Shield during the 1980s. Name them. *Four points*

12 From which province did 1980–81 All Black Andy Jefferd become an All Black? *One point*

13 Which team won the inaugural national championship first division in 1976? *One point*

14 In what year did All Black captain Graham Mourie retire from international rugby? *One point*

15 Name the All Black whose autobiography was called *Pieces of Eight*. *One point*

16 A total of five All Blacks crossed over to rugby league during the 1990 season. Name them. *Five points*

17 Which unions play for the Seddon Shield? *Four points*

18 Name the only All Black to ever be sent home from an overseas tour. *One point*

19 Who captained the All Blacks on the 1986 tour of France? *One point*

20 Colin Meads played for the All Blacks from 1957–71. How many appearances did he make: (a) 91; (b) 106; (c) 133; (d) 157? *One point*

21 Who was tour captain of the 1986 Cavaliers team to South Africa? *One point*

22 In what year did the points value of a try increase from three points to four points? *One point*

23 Bryan Williams, an All Black from 1970–78, holds the record for most tries for New Zealand. How many did he score: (a) 50; (b) 66; (c) 72; (d) 93? *One point*

24 Only one team beat Auckland during the 1989 season. Who was it? *One point*

25 Name the All Black prop who kicked a conversion on the 1972–73 tour of the United Kingdom and France. *One point*

26 Three members of the All Blacks World Cup squad did not play a game. Name them. *Three points*

27 How old was John Kirwan when he became an All Black? *One point*

28 All Black prop Richard Loe represented two South Island provinces before reaching Waikato. Name them. *Two points*

29 Who scored 201 points in test rugby between 1981 and 1984? *One point*

30 What South African province did All Black lock Murray Pierce represent in 1990? *One point*

31 Name the coaches of Canterbury, Waikato, North Auckland and Taranaki during the 1990 season. *Four points*

32 Andy Leslie, All Black captain from 1974 to 1976, represented New Zealand at what other sport? *One point*

33 Who replaced Zinzan Brooke when he left the field in the second half of the second test against Australia in 1990? *One point*

34 "Tiny" Hill, an All Black from 1955 to 1959, has two sons who played basketball for New Zealand. What are their christian names? *Two points*

35 Five players have made more than 100 appearances for the All Blacks. Name them. *Five points*

36 Who holds the record for most points in all matches for New Zealand? *One point*

37 Which player has captained New Zealand the most often in test matches? *One point*

38 Who captained the All Blacks to Scotland and England in 1983? *One point*

39 The All Blacks' highest score in a test match was against Fiji in the 1987 World Cup. Score please. *One point*

40 Whose record did John Kirwan break when he became the leading tryscorer in test matches for New Zealand in the first test against Australia in 1988? *One point*

41 Name the All Black tryscorers in the World Cup final against France in 1987. *Three points*

42 Name the 1988 Welsh first-five who returned to New Zealand with the British rugby league team in 1990. *One point*

43 What was the nickname given to the All Black team that played France at Lancaster Park in 1986? *One point*

44 The 1986 Australian tourists lost only one provincial game. To who? *One point*

45 The All Blacks called for two replacements on the 1989 tour of Wales and Ireland. Who were they and who did they replace? *Four points*

46 Name the player who made his test debut replacing Frano Botica with a minute to play in the third test against Australia in 1986. *One point*

47 Name the selected fullback who pulled out before the first test against Scotland in 1981 and never got to play for the All Blacks. *One point*

48 When did New Zealand first win the Hong Kong sevens? *One point*

49 Only one team other than the All Blacks beat the 1977 British Lions. Who? *One point*

50 Which famous All Black coach was nicknamed "Needle"? *One point*

51 Name the two brothers of former All Black halfback Sid Going who were top players in their own right. *Two points*

52 When was the last North Island–South Island match played? *One point*

53 A 1920s Hawkes Bay player held the record for most tries in Ranfurly Shield rugby until this year. Name him. *One point*

54 Who won the national championship third division in 1990? *One point*

55 In what country was 1979–84 All Black winger Bernie Fraser born? *One point*

56 In what year was the North Harbour Union founded? *One point*

57 Who did Marlborough take the Ranfurly Shield from in 1973? *One point*

58 One of the following unions — South Canterbury, Southland, Bay of Plenty and Taranaki — has never held the Ranfurly Shield. Which one? *One point*

59 Name the woman journalist who has worked for *Rugby News* in recent years. *One point*

60 Name the three All Black selectors. *Three points*

61 Name the former New Zealand Secondary Schools representative who returned to New Zealand with the 1990 Australian team. *One point*

62 Which Auckland club did Matthew Ridge play for before converting to rugby league? *One point*

63 Who scored New Zealand's only try in the second test against Scotland in 1990? *One point*

64 Waikato centre Matthew Cooper made one tour with the All Blacks. To where and when? *Two points*

65 Who captained New Zealand in the 1978 test series against Australia? *One point*

66 How many times has Wellington won the national championship? *One point*

67 Name the Taranaki winger on the 1985 All Black tour to Argentina. *One point*

68 What is the most number of tries scored by an individual in a match for the All Blacks? *One point*

69 Which one of Earle Kirton, Grant Batty, Gary Knight and Albert Anderson won a Commonwealth Games medal? *One point*

70 Romania have toured New Zealand only once. When? *One point*

71 Who played the first of his 24 tests at halfback for New Zealand against Wales in 1978? *One point*

72 All Black prop Richard Loe is a nephew of All Black coach Alex Wyllie. True or false? *One point*

73 Who kicked a last minute penalty to give New Zealand victory over Wales in 1978? *One point*

74 The present race relations conciliator is a former All Black. Name him. *One point*

75 Who played all 32 games on the All Blacks' 1924–25 tour of the United Kingdom, France and Canada? *One point*

76 Name the brilliant 1981–85 All Black back who retired from the Wellington representative team in 1990. *One point*

77 What is the name given to the United States rugby team? *One point*

78 Name the 1980s All Black and 1990 Development Squad assistant coach who had the nickname "Cowboy". *One point*

79 Three players in the 1990 Otago backline have played for the All Blacks. Name them. *Three points*

80 Who captained the 1990 New Zealand Colts? *One point*

81 What device was introduced in 1990 to save kickers time? *One point*

82 Name the All Black flanker who was Hawkes Bay captain in the 1960. *One point*

83 Name the North Auckland brothers who were wingers in New Zealand teams in the early 1980s. *Two points*

84 Which one of these teams — Mid-Canterbury, Poverty Bay, Nelson Bays and King Country — was not in second division in 1990? *One point*

85 Name the former All Black halfback who coached Manawatu in 1990. *One point*

86 Who won the 1990 Hong Kong sevens? *One point*

87 Name the vice-captain on the All Black tour of Wales and Ireland in 1989. *One point*

88 Name the 1989 New Zealand Secondary Schools player who became a 1990 All Black. *One point*

89 Where did Auckland take the Ranfurly Shield on tour in 1990? *One point*

90 Name North Auckland's home ground. *One point*

91 Two players scored four tries in the All Blacks victory against Fiji in the 1987 World Cup. Who? *Two points*

92 Auckland drew one national championship game in 1989. Against who? *One point*

93 Which player has played the most successive tests for New Zealand? *One point*

94 Who was the 1981 All Black who returned to New Zealand in 1985 with the England team? *One point*

95 Name the Australian player who has scored more points in test matches against New Zealand than any other international player. *One point*

96 When New Zealand drew with Argentina 21–21 in 1985 who scored all of the Argentinians' points? *One point*

97 Which one of these teams — Counties, North Auckland, Canterbury and Manawatu — has never won the national championship? *One point*

98 When Waikato lifted the Ranfurly Shield from Auckland in 1980 who scored their runaway try? *One point*

99 Name the Otago halfback who often kept David Kirk on the sideline in 1983 and 1984? *One point*

100 Who did South Africa draw with on their 1981 tour of New Zealand? *One point*

ANSWERS ON PAGE 136

Grant Harding is a journalist who was the researcher for the successful television series *Mud and Glory*. He was a *Mastermind* finalist in 1989.

THE ALL BLACKS' MOST DRAMATIC TEST

By BOB HOWITT

NEW ZEALAND 25
SOUTH AFRICA 22
Eden Park
Auckland
September 12, 1981

"That was quite an afternoon's entertainment," observed a spectator as he took his exit from the main grandstand at Eden Park. "For $12 we got a cracking rugby international, a fireworks display and an air pageant!"

Not everyone shared his enthusiasm for the spectacular events of the day.

Not, for example, the elite Red Squad of the New Zealand Police force who had sent Andy Dalton's men a telegram of encouragement.

"Good luck," read the telegram. "We'll be outside and will only know how you're faring from the cheering."

While the test raged inside Eden Park, the Red Squad became locked in an ugly confrontation with protestors in Sandringham Road and adjoining streets. The worst violence of the tour ensued, with rocks, road signs and fence posts being thrown. Many individuals from both sides were injured, some seriously.

The players themselves found the happenings unsettling. They almost had this momentous sporting occasion ruined by the pilot of a Cessna who buzzed the ground incessantly throughout the test — making more than 60 low, distracting sweeps — dropping flour bombs, leaflets and even some flares.

Gary Knight certainly didn't appreciate it. He was struck in the face by a flour bomb and knocked to the ground. Fortunately, he was only stunned and was able to continue playing.

The thousands of spectators sitting in the numbers six and seven stands most certainly could have done without the "air pageant".

They held their breaths each time the pilot cut his engine to drop close to the field, knowing that only a slight miscalculation could have the Cessna plummeting in among them.

Former All Black Ron Rangi, who had participated in the series triumph against the previous Springbok touring team, in 1965, was one who could take no more than 40 minutes of bombardment from above. At halftime he left, visibly shaken, unprepared to sit through another session in the firing line.

Commissioner of Police Bob Walton didn't enjoy the afternoon one little bit. He had to assess the danger the low-flying plane presented and weigh that danger against the violence that would have eventuated had tens of thousands of angry spectators poured out of the stadium and confronted the demonstrators if he abandoned the game.

The South African radio and television commentators regarded the occasion as the most frustrating of their lives.

The cutting of microwave cables near Warkworth — presumably as a protest against the Springboks' presence in New Zealand — meant all their lines to South Africa went dead and they were unable to commentate.

South African Broadcasting Corporation commentator Trevor Quirk summed it up: "Probably the biggest sporting occasion any of us could report on to South Africa — and all we could do was sit and watch."

South Africa, incidentally, didn't miss out altogether but the only commentary which got through — via satellite — was that by Keith Quinn and Grahame Thorne, accompanying the New Zealand TV picture.

It was, to be sure, a most remarkable occasion, one which will never be forgotten by any of those present.

The 1956 Eden Park test is remembered for Peter Jones' epic charge to the tryline; the 1965 test for the manner in which Colin Meads and a mighty forward pack set up a record victory against the Springboks.

But 1981 will be remembered for many things — the dive-bombing plane, the flares, the barbed wire, Gary Knight being struck by a flour bomb, the Springboks' comeback from 3–16 to 22–all, how Naas Botha sliced the last conversion, how Allan Hewson slotted the winning penalty and the "long" last five minutes.

It was billed in some quarters as the test of the century. For reasons not altogether rugby, that's probably a fair description.

The sensations began in the days leading up to the contest but this time the agonies came in the Springbok camp.

New Zealand had a changed team from Wellington but it was mostly of the selectors' own making. Two of the heroes of the Maoris' performance in Napier had been introduced — second-five Steve Pokere and flanker Frank Shelford — and the promising young Auckland lock Gary Whetton had been chosen to partner Andy Haden, ahead of veteran Frank Oliver.

Mark Shaw was named in the side but withdrew early in the week because the hip injury which had bothered him against Scotland was still dogging him. The selectors, after a lengthy deliberation, decided that Geoff Old, a specialist No 8, should be chosen to play as the blindside flanker.

To accommodate Pokere, winger Fred Woodman had been relegated to the reserves, with Lachlan Cameron and Stu Wilson each moving out a place.

South Africa suffered two crushing setbacks in the 48 hours before kick-off. First, De Villiers Visser, the second rower who had performed so heroically at Athletic Park, dropped out with a rib injury and on the morning of the match Theuns Stofberg cried off with a wonky knee.

These injuries effectively removed South Africa's two best driving forwards of the second test and significantly lessened the tourists' hopes of pulling off victory.

Rob Louw and Hennie Bekker were the substitutes, Louw going to the side of the scrum and Bekker locking with Louis Moolman.

These, forced, changes were the only ones from the team which had so handsomely won the second test.

Test day dawned bright and sunny but if the weather was immeasurably better, the tension was as gripping as it had been in Wellington.

Eden Park was a sellout and latecomers were having difficulty purchasing tickets. The crowd, said Auckland union chairman Ron Don, would be 49,000, capacity for the day. Protestors, their organisers claimed, would number more than 5000 and they were asembling much earlier than for the Auckland game the previous Saturday.

Those who took themselves to Eden Park early experienced no difficulties getting in; in fact, they needed some convincing that anything untoward (other than the buzzing of the Cessna) occurred anywhere near the Park that day.

But latecomers struck difficulties getting past the human barricades formed by the protestors. Some filed through narrow channels forged by the police; others were diverted through private properties.

These were the nearby problems. Others had been delayed when the Harbour Bridge was blocked. Obviously most rugby fans circumnavigated the barriers because there were precious few empty seats when Welshman Clive Norling — an impressive figure indeed in his bright red jersey — signalled the start of play at 2.30pm.

In Wellington Andy Dalton, having won the toss, invited the Springboks to take first advantage of the wind, a decision he came to regret. At Eden Park Wynand Claassen having won the toss returned the compliment. And he, too, lived to regret it. Though in Claassen's case it was more than just the wind which influenced events; for the first 40 minutes his players had to face the flour bomb assault from above.

"I would never have agreed to play into the wind if I had appreciated what was coming," said Claassen. "Throughout that first spell my players were half concentrating on the game, half worrying about the plane.

"I know it became New Zealand's problem in the second spell but by then New Zealand had sixteen points on the board and I think the longer the pilot went on the less we worried about him."

Psychology plays a big part in top-level rugby and it was easy to trace in all three tests. In Christchurch the All Blacks had been wound up to produce their best. Two weeks later the desperate 'Boks were motivated to the heavens. At Eden Park it was the All Blacks again, breathing fire.

The forwards were just magnificent, led by Gary Knight (what a difference his return meant to the front row), Andy Haden and new boy Gary Whetton, who amazed everyone by matching Louis Moolman in the lineouts.

After Allan Hewson and Naas Botha had traded penalty goals New Zealand scored just about the sweetest try of the entire series.

It came directly from the kick-off that followed Botha's penalty, Knight securing the ball and driving determinedly upfield.

When the ball came back Pokere was, somehow, at first-five with Rollerson out at centre. Anyway, super-slick passes from both of them expedited the ball to Hewson who exploded into the backline outside Rollerson and burst through into the clear.

Hewson was to commit some major blunders before this contest was through but his achievement in setting up this first try was magical. He bluffed Gysie Pienaar into believing he was going to pass but straightened the attack and surged onward, delaying his pass perfectly to give Wilson the best possible scoring opportunity. That was all Super Stu needed. His pace took him away from Botha, who was covering, and a huge sidestep took him inside Ray Mordt and across the goalline for his sixth test try of the season.

There was another champion try before halftime, this one the work of the forwards, Murray Mexted detaching and hurling himself towards the line from a five metre scrum. The 'Boks halted him but as the ball spewed clear Knight snapped it up and plunged across.

By this stage the left-footed Hewson

ANDY HADEN leads the All Blacks in a stirring charge against the Springboks at Eden Park in the unforgettable final test. Gary Whetton, who was making his test debut, provides back-up.   Photo by : PETER BUSH

TOP: Barbed wire very much in evidence as winger Ray Mordt goes in for the try that levelled the scores at 22-all.
ABOVE: The final whistle, New Zealand ahead 25-22 and time to celebrate. Photos by : PETER BUSH and WESSEL OOSTHUIZEN

was taking the kicks from the right-hand side of the field and Rollerson those from the left.

Between them they succeeded three times during the spell, giving New Zealand an overwhelming (and obviously a matchwinning) advantage of 16–3 at the turnaround.

A matchwinning lead? The 'Boks had come back from 5–16 to win in Christchurch in 1965 and they were determined to supersede that this time.

The second half belonged to the right winger Ray Mordt, the former Rhodesian who was the only one of the 32 tourists not proficient in Afrikaans. But he was sure proficient in tryscoring.

In the fifth and 12th minutes he took tries at the expense of Hewson, outsprinting him for the first after Colin Beck (on as a sub for Willie du Plessis)

had placed a perfect kick through to the tryline and gratefully snatching the second after Hewson had hesitated and allowed Mordt's own kick ahead to bounce.

Botha conversions brought the 'Boks up to 18–19 with still 22 minutes to play. The crowd was simmering.

A Doug Rollerson dropped goal, after a stampeding run by Haden, put New Zealand four points ahead and the crowd breathed again. Now it needed a try by the Springboks. And time was running out.

With a minute showing on the clock the Springbok backs attacked but Beck was chopped down in midfield by Cameron. As the ball spilled free Bernie Fraser tried a speculator which missed and Botha showed himself to be the superior

soccer player, toeing the ball ahead, then gathering it in and stepping clear of frantic tackles by Mexted and Pokere to put Mordt across for try No 3.

What a fairytale finish! The clock showed fulltime and it was 22–22, Botha's sideline conversion to come. But poor Naas had to stew for at least two minutes while Loveridge, concussed trying to stop Mordt, was carried off. While this was happening the Cessna roared through on its lowest, most daring, sweep of the day.

Finally, Botha got the okay to kick. Forty-eight thousand New Zealanders in the stadium (the other thousand were South Africans) *knew* the kick was going over. This was the man who had slotted four out of four already that afternoon and who had maintained a 75 per cent success rate throughout the tour.

REFEREE Clive Norling signals a try to All Black prop Gary Knight, witnessed by flanker Frank Shelford. It was quite a day for Knight who was struck by a flour bomb from above.   Photo by : PETER BUSH

SPRINGBOK flyhalf Naas Botha runs through the tackle of Steven Pokere at a tense stage of the Eden Park test.

Photo by : PETER BUSH

But he didn't swing round quite enough on his kick, pushing it to the right of the uprights.

So, a 22–22 draw. What a fitting result for this besieged tour. A tied series, as in 1921.

Now what the crowd didn't know was that about 10 minutes earlier referee Norling had asked the rival skippers if they wanted to make up all the time lost for such off-beat stoppages as flour bombings, flares going off etc.

Both captains had said yes. So when Botha's kick missed there were still about five minutes to play — which the crowd didn't know about.

Play resumed. The Springboks won two lineouts, both times clearing to touch. Still no final whistle. Then a scrum 36 metres out from the Springbok posts, Springbok put-in.

Serfontein, who'd done everything right all afternoon, baulked the feed, causing his hooker Robert Cockrell to strike early. Referee Norling duly awarded a free kick to New Zealand.

Mark Donaldson, who'd come on for Loveridge (not really expecting to get more than a few seconds' action) took a quick tap penalty and charged upfield only to be tackled.

However, referee Norling ruled that the Springbok threequarters had not retired the required 10 metres, so he returned to the mark and awarded a penalty.

Everything hung on that final kick. Hewson took it because it was on the right-hand side of the field.

"I kept saying to myself, 'It has to go over. It has to go over.' Then I blanked everything out of my mind and just concentrated on kicking accurately. The kick felt good and I can't tell you how good I felt watching it curl inside the upright. I knew then we'd beaten the Springboks."

Less than a minute later the whistle went for fulltime, New Zealand ahead 25–22 in one of the most amazing test matches ever played. ∎

Bob Howitt has been editor of *Rugby News* and the *New Zealand Rugby Annual* since their inceptions 20 years ago. Among New Zealand's most prolific writers he has followed almost every All Black tour since the mid-1960s.

NEW ZEALAND'S GREATEST PROVINCIAL MATCH

By BOB HOWITT

Alex Wyllie collected a ball as he walked into the middle of Lancaster Park at halftime, his champion side in tatters at 24–nil down.

"This," he said, holding the ball in front of his demoralised players, "is what it's all about. Get it and use it.

"If Auckland could score twenty-four points in that half using it, you can score twenty-four points in the second."

He said no more. He walked deliberately back to the grandstand, still believing his team, which had destroyed all comers to Lancaster Park for three magnificent seasons, could salvage the game.

"We're as good a team as Auckland," he said later. "There was no reason to believe we couldn't produce in the second half what they produced in the first."

And how despairingly close this great Canterbury team came to pulling off what would have ranked as the greatest comeback triumph surely in the entire history of the game in this country.

After Albert Anderson had launched himself up and over a desperate defence for a spectacular try Canterbury had achieved the impossible of cutting a 24-point deficit to just five. And two and a half minutes still remained.

Suddenly the vast crowd, who had watched in stunned silence through the first half as Auckland mercilessly piled on the points, was in pandemonium. A converted try would do it.

In identical circumstances hadn't Auckland stolen the most dramatic of Ranfurly Shield victories, off Canterbury, 25 years earlier, when Waka Nathan crossed the goalline and ran round behind the posts for Mike Cormack to convert, for a 19–18 victory with time up on the clock?

Auckland did it then. Canterbury could do it now.

And oh how they tried. They were rampant. Auckland confused and desperate, unable to comprehend that a match so secure might now be wrenched from them.

A final lineout, 40 metres from the Auckland tryline. Canterbury's ball. Then the inevitable, on an afternoon when "bombs" had created such chaos and so many tries . . . a soaring up-and-under from Wayne Smith.

Those final few seconds seemed to be acted out in slow motion.

The blue and white jerseys were grouped, waiting, seemingly half a dozen men each determined to claim the ball and thwart this final raid.

But the red jerseys bore down upon them like a military charge from which there would be no survivors. The ball bobbled on finger tips and through its own momentum cannoned down into the rock-hard turf and bounced high behind the goalline.

Jock Hobbs, the Canterbury flanker, captured the agony of the next few agonising instants when he said that that moment would be frozen in his memory for ever.

"Everything seemed to be happening in slow motion," he said. "The ball was there for them, for us, but like in a nightmare it stayed tantalisingly inches beyond our grasp."

John Kirwan, at full stretch, just managed to reach the ball and nudge it to safety beyond the deadball line.

Had he missed and the ball dropped behind him, Canterbury's replacement back Wayne Burleigh would have been presented with a try. Then everything would have hinged on Robbie Deans' close-range conversion attempt and what delirium would have ensued then.

But Kirwan's effort was enough to win the Ranfurly Shield for Auckland, for upon seeing the ball go dead, referee Bob Francis signalled the finish of the game.

This was billed as the provincial match of the century and, incredibly, it lived up to that.

There was a lot of the unreal about the game.

A couple of Auckland's first spell tries were unreal.

That either of these two mighty teams could establish a 24-point advantage over the other was unreal.

And that any team could come back from 24 points down (twice, at 0–24 and 4–28) with the advantage of only a light breeze was very definitely unreal.

Canterbury should never have had to stage such a barnstorming finish to retrieve its desperate situation.

It fired the shield away during a calamitous opening 24 minutes when All Blacks Robbie Deans and Vic Simpson were guilty of enormous blunders.

Deans, so often the hero during Canterbury's shield reign, dropped one of Grant Fox's early "bombs", yielding a ruck from which Joe Stanley scored for Fox to convert.

And Simpson, possibly frustrated by Auckland's magnificent defence, yielded to impulse and sought to counter attack from inside his 22, was promptly gobbled up by at least two Auckland raiders and in a flash John Kirwan was across in the corner.

Terry Wright scored a freakish tearaway try, which only his extreme pace made possible, and John Drake plunged through for a boomer after another Kirwan sideline break.

John Hart was far from happy at halftime, alarmed that Auckland would become complacent and knowing Can-

AUCKLANDERS Sean Fitzpatrick, left, Terry Wright and Steve McDowell received a heroes welcome when they returned home from Christchurch in 1985 bearing the Ranfurly Shield.   Photo by : AUCKLAND STAR

terbury would rally.

It did but Auckland's 24-point advantage saw it through to the finish.

Auckland's heroes were many and not the least of them was Hart himself, who masterminded a low-key build-up and tactics that finally overcame the red and black goliath.

Steve McDowell deservedly won the player of the match award, for his contribution was immense, in the scrums, rucks and mauls; Andy Haden and Gary Whetton controlled the lineouts for three-quarters of the match (Canterbury salvaging something only when lanky Pat O'Gorman replaced Dale Atkins); Glenn Rich won lineout ball and stood off the scrums to block every Atkins charge; while Mark Brooke-Cowden tackled heroically all afternoon and made several telling charges.

Joe Stanley was probably the mightiest of all Auckland's backs, with his thrust and telling first-time tackling of Simpson; Grant Fox and David Kirk made massive contributions; Kurt Sherlock tackled his heart out; Kirwan twice cracked the defence for tries; and Wright showed his exceptional skills in tryscoring and covering.

For Canterbury, a nightmare first 40 minutes riddled with errors, then a heroic and magnificent comeback, in which Bruce Deans, Wayne Smith, skipper Don Hayes and Jock Hobbs were irresistible.

It really was the provincial game of the century.   ■

Bob Howitt has been editor of *Rugby News* and the *New Zealand Rugby Annual* since their inceptions 20 years ago. Among New Zealand's most prolific writers he has followed almost every All Black tour since the mid-1960s.

A3

Pete McLauchlan, cartoonist, lives in Geraldine and plays golden oldie rugby there for the Ruakapuka Roosters.
He much earlier achieved fame as the first player in Southland to wear a nose guard,
completing his first game concussed.

THE ALL BLACKS' MOST EXCITING FINISH

By BOB HOWITT

NEW ZEALAND 32
QUAGGA–
BARBARIANS 31
Ellis Park
Johannesburg
August 18, 1976

"When I saw the scoreboard reading thirty-one to nine with twenty minutes to go I thought, 'My God, we're going to lose this by fifty points'," confessed All Black skipper Andy Leslie after piloting his side through the most remarkable comeback victory in the history of international rugby.

"I couldn't think of anything to say at that stage," said Leslie. "So I just told the boys to forget about me and do their best."

At 9–31 the team had already conceded more points than any All Black side before them and the New Zealand journalists in the press box were flicking through record books to establish the heaviest defeat ever suffered by New Zealand.

The journos never completed the exercise.

Within a minute the All Blacks had started their comeback extraordinary.

They scored, in fact, from the kick-off through a surprise kick to the right. It had produced the All Blacks' only try in the first test and it worked again here, Bruce Robertson and Terry Mitchell combining for Mitchell to score.

That quick try which, with Laurie Mains' conversion took the score to 31–15, made the All Blacks believe they could win.

And so started the comeback of comebacks — one which produced four tries and 22 points in 26 minutes.

To the astonishment of the huge midweek crowd who had roared with delight as the Quagga-Barbarians team, through delightful running rugby against some flimsy defence, piled on the points, the All Blacks took off.

A penalty to Mains; a try to Sutherland.

Into injury time, the Quagga-Barbarians ahead 31–22.

A try to Lawrie Knight, converted by Mains, 31–28.

Time must be up, it seems, but the referee Steve Strydom returns to halfway for the kick-off, where Leslie approaches him and asks, "How long to go?"

"Twenty-nine seconds," says Strydom.

Leslie returns to the All Blacks and, not wanting to panic them, tells them there are three minutes left to play.

From the kick-off the ball goes into touch. There are now only 10 to 15 seconds left.

The Quaggas win the lineout and flyhalf Gavin Cowley who has enjoyed an outstanding attacking game prefers not to boot into touch but goes for another try.

The Quaggas surge towards the New Zealand posts and for a moment it seems their fifth try is on the way.

But as the defence rallies five metres out Quaggas skipper Salty du Rand rises up and throws a big pass to his backs.

Leslie, who has been lurking outside the 10-metre area, anticipates brilliantly what is happening and swoops, intercepting the ball.

He's away upfield but he doesn't like his chances of outrunning the speedsters for 85 metres — so he kicks ahead. A perfect kick. It rolls and rolls and torments the Quaggas men who try to get it under control. The All Blacks toe it on.

Finally, fullback Ian Robertson gets it in his grasp on his 22-metre line. A quick kick to touch and the Quaggas have won.

But before he can even get his right foot off the ground to kick, he is gunned down by Bruce Robertson and the ball rolls free.

"I don't know why every forward chased the ball so desperately from the other end of the field," said hooker Graeme Crossman later, "but we did."

The full pack was there to charge into the ruck, just out from the Quaggas posts. The ball took an agonising time to come back and it seemed Ref Strydom may even signal for a scrum and thus end the game.

But finally the ball plopped out. Lyn Davis, in his haste to clear it, rolled his pass along the ground and almost had it intercepted but Duncan Robertson got it and fired it on. Out, out, out it went, to Terry Mitchell who had the overlap and waltzed across untouched for the match-winner.

What a finish! What a game! The All Blacks reacted with greater emotion than they had at the conclusion of their great second test victory.

There have been comebacks and comebacks but to get from 9–31 to 32–31 in the final quarter was, indeed, as one journalist put it, "an impossible victory".

The Quagga-Baabaas side, which included Irishmen Fergus Slattery and Tom Grace (who both played exceedingly well) had led 10–0 after 16 minutes and was up 13–9 at halftime.

Then, in 11 sensational minutes, the home side ran in three converted tries — by Grace, threequarter Joe Coetser and replacement flanker Corrie Pypers.

The Quaggas could thank their No 8 Johan Claassen and inside backs Dave Zietsman and Gavin Cowley for this stunning advantage. All three had magnificent games and seemed to be able to run through the New Zealand defence as if it was non-existent.

The All Black comeback was the more remarkable because at 31–9 the Quagga-

Baabaas seemed completely in charge of the game.

"Just put it down to team spirit," commented an elated All Black after it was all over. "We couldn't let JJ Stewart down that badly." ∎

WINGER Terry Mitchell, tackled here by Pierre Goosen (12), scored the last-second try that brought the All Blacks their sensational victory over the South African Barbarians. The other Baabaas player is Dave Zietsman.

Photo by : WESSEL OOSTHUIZEN

Bob Howitt has been editor of *Rugby News* and the *New Zealand Rugby Annual* since their inceptions 20 years ago. Among New Zealand's most prolific writers he has followed almost every All Black tour since the mid-1960s.

NEW ZEALAND'S MOST CONTROVERSIAL TEST WIN

By BOB HOWITT

NEW ZEALAND 13
WALES 12
Arms Park
Cardiff
November 11, 1978

One of Wales' most ardent fans is actor Richard Burton. It was a shame he couldn't be at the Arms Park for this contest because Hollywood acting contributed to the final result almost as much as did pure rugby.

The Welsh backs feigned obstruction several times in the first half, drawing penalties that helped the side build a 12–7 halftime advantage.

But these efforts were forgotten when New Zealand's two beefy locks Andy Haden and Frank Oliver grabbed the spotlight in the final seconds with Wales ahead 12–10.

Obviously reasoning that victory over arch rival Wales could be justified by fair means or foul, neither Haden nor Oliver jumped in what was in all probability going to be the game's final lineout.

What they did instead was to act as though their Welsh opponents had inflicted terrible obstruction upon them.

Haden cartwheeled sidewards in farcical style, leading most spectators to believe he was the victim of some fearful barging by his marker Allan Martin. Television later revealed that no one laid a hand on Haden.

Oliver was more subtle. He merely turned sideways and threw his arms in the air. Whether referee Roger Quittenton would have taken any notice of Oliver's act (he didn't even see Haden doing his thing) will never be known, because by a great twist of irony the Welsh lock Geoff Wheel genuinely infringed — and was penalised.

Wheel needlessly pushed himself off Oliver's shoulder as he rose to win the ball, an infringement that Quittenton had no option but to penalise.

The Welsh crowd was stunned. Their team, which had not defeated the All Blacks since 1953, had been ahead since the fifth minute, and had seemed assured of victory as it exerted great pressure on New Zealand until these final few hectic moments.

Now everything rested on the goalkick by Brian McKechnie.

The odds on McKechnie even being on the field were about a thousand to one.

Not originally selected, he joined Mourie's Men on tour only when Bevan Wilson suffered a grim knee injury.

He came into the reserves for the Welsh test only when Mark Donaldson cried off on the Friday and he got on to the Arms Park only because Clive Currie was concussed in a heavy tackle from Steve Fenwick.

Super-cool McKechnie placed goals in the 39th and 55th minutes to put New Zealand within striking distance and here was his chance to achieve everlasting fame.

"As I walked up to it, a few terrifying thoughts raced through my mind," said McKechnie " — the usual panic feeling. But as I made my mark I felt calm and confident.

"I was determined it would be a quick kick. The longer you take, the more aware you become of the tension and all the things that can go wrong."

McKechnie's kick was dead between the posts, giving New Zealand the lead for the only time in this dramatic contest played in an atmosphere that was electric.

This was the second injury-time test victory in a week for Mourie's team, to the chagrin of 50,000 Welsh fans, who at the final whistle could not believe the match had been stolen from them.

BRIAN McKECHNIE gets the okay to replace Clive Currie at Cardiff in 1978. The odds against him participating in this match were a thousand to one.

Photo by : PETER BUSH

ALL BLACKS Billy Bush, left, goalkicking hero McKechnie and Leicester Rutledge look more stunned than elated after the victory over Wales.

Photo by : PETER BUSH

New Zealand won, in the final count, because it scored a try and Wales didn't and because New Zealand's backs were decisively superior to their opposites.

With super-charged Welsh forwards surprisingly winning not only the line-outs but the rucks as well, Wales had 60 per cent possession but couldn't use it. Several times the Welsh backs found themselves with a three-to-one situation, only to blunder.

New Zealand's try was a gem, the product of a clever kick by Dave Loveridge to put the All Blacks on attack, furious rucking by the forwards and a superb kick through by Bill Osborne which flying Stu Wilson got to first.

Loveridge enjoyed an excellent test debut, inspiring some grand football from Osborne, Bruce Robertson and Stu Wilson.

Foolish late charges (fully capitalised on by the Welsh) and a needless punch by Frank Oliver almost fired this test away.

But Mourie's Men showed their spirit and tenacity to chalk up test victory number two. ∎

THE fateful kick, a few moments before fulltime. McKechnie slotted it for a desperate one-point All Black test victory.

Photo by : PETER BUSH

Bob Howitt has been editor of *Rugby News* and the *New Zealand Rugby Annual* since their inceptions 20 years ago. Among New Zealand's most prolific writers he has followed almost every All Black tour since the mid-1960s.

PROFILE : TIM GAVIN

Full name: Bryant Timothy Gavin.
Birthdate: November 20, 1963.
Zodiac sign: Scorpio.
Birthplace: Gilgandra, New South Wales.
Residence: Cumnock, New South Wales.
Occupation: Farmer.
Height: 1.97m.
Weight: 107kg.
Marital status: Single.
Position: No 8.
Present club: Eastern Suburbs, Sydney.
Most difficult opponent: Wayne Shelford.
Best rugby memory: Third test victory over the All Blacks in 1990.
Biggest disappointment: Losing 1990 club grand final.
Favourite country: United States.
Biggest influence on career: My father telling me not to come home until I'd played for Australia!
Other sports/leisure interests: Fishing, guitar.
Favourite rugby ground: Murrayfield.
Favourite film: *World According to Garp.*
Favourite TV show: *Big Country Australian Show.*
Favourite music: Rolling Stones.
Favourite food: Mum's.
Funniest rugby experience: Any game against Fiji.
Biggest drag in rugby: Always training; plane travel.

PROFILE : JOHN JEFFREY

Full name: John Jeffrey.
Birthdate: March 25, 1959.
Zodiac sign: Aries.
Birthplace: Kelso.
Residence: Kersknowe, Kelso, Scotland.
Occupation: Farmer.
Height: 1.93m.
Weight: 91kg.
Marital status: Single.
Years playing rugby: Since being able to walk!
Position: Back row.
Present club: Kelso.
International experience: 30 caps for Scotland; 1 British Lions cap.
Most difficult opponent: Mark "Cowboy" Shaw.
Best rugby memory: 1987 World Cup in New Zealand.
Most memorable match: Scotland versus England, Murrayfield 1986.
Biggest disappointment: Being injured and missing the quarter-final against New Zealand in the World Cup.
Favourite country: Bermuda.
Biggest influence on career: Gary Callander.
Other sports/leisure interests: Golf, skiing, water-skiing.
Favourite rugby ground: Murrayfield.
Favourite films: Videos of Scotland hammering England!
Favourite TV shows: Sport, *Fawlty Towers*, *Aufwiedersen Pet*.
Favourite music: All kinds of popular music.
Favourite food: Any meat.
Funniest rugby experience: Erica Roe's performance at Twickenham.
Biggest drag in rugby: Training in bad weather.

PROFILE : MICHAEL LYNAGH

Full name: Michael Patrick Thomas Lynagh.

Birthdate: October 25, 1963.
Zodiac sign: Scorpio.
Birthplace: Brisbane.
Residence: Brisbane.
Occupation: Manager for Robt Jones Investments.
Height: 1.78m.
Weight: 78kg.
Marital status: Single.
Position: First-five.
Present club: University of Queensland.
Most difficult opponent: Any All Black.
Best rugby memories: 1984 Grand Slam tour; 1986 tour to New Zealand — third test.
Biggest disappointment: Losing.
Favourite country: United States.
Biggest influence on career: My father, Ian.
Other sports/leisure interests: Golf, surfing; reading.
Favourite rugby ground: Sydney Football Stadium.
Favourite film: *One Flew Over the Cuckoo's Nest* stands out from many great movies.
Favourite TV shows: *The Wonder Years*; also enjoy watching golf and good comedy.
Favourite music: The Saints, The Chills.
Favourite food: Seafood, hot spicy foods such as Mexican or curries.
Funniest rugby experience: Happy hour after Australia and Queensland games would rate as being constantly funny over the years.
Biggest drag in rugby: Being away from home; getting injured.

PROFILE : GRANT FOX

Full name: Grant James Fox.
Birthdate: June 16, 1962.
Zodiac sign: Gemini.
Birthplace: New Plymouth.
Residence: Auckland.
Occupation: Sports Marketing.
Height: 1.75m.
Weight: 77kg.
Marital status: Married with two children.
Position: First-five.
Present club: University.
Most difficult opponent: The next one.
Best rugby memories: Playing test matches; winning the World Cup.
Biggest disappointment: Cancellation of 1985 All Black tour to South Africa.
Favourite countries: South Africa; Argentina.
Biggest influence on career: Too many to mention.
Other sports/leisure interests: Cricket, golf, tennis; my family.
Favourite rugby ground: Eden Park.
Favourite films: *Top Gun, Good Morning Vietnam.*
Favourite TV shows: *Cheers, Married With Children.*
Favourite music: Easy listening.
Favourite food: Roast lamb.
Funniest rugby experience: Playing in the same team as John McDermott.
Biggest drag in rugby: Cold showers; the waiting before games.

MARTY 'N' ZINZAN 'N' ROBIN AND THE TEAM

By DENIS EDWARDS

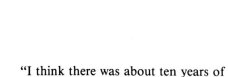

Making it to the top in sport takes time, talent, tenacity, plenty of support and a will to win bordering on the obsessive.

The Brooke brothers, or most of them, are blessed with these attributes. It has paid off for them as the Brooke family is right up at the peak of this country's rugby.

Not only are they filling the Auckland and, in Zinzan's case, the All Black scrum but also they provide replacements for each other.

The best example was Marty's departure for a two-year stint in Japan. No problem. Robin was right there, ready, willing and able to keep the Auckland rolling maul moving right along.

Close behind, dropping on the ball for a phenomenal number of tries, is Zinzan. His unusual first name is taken from his grandmother's maiden name.

Zinzan Brooke had a lengthy wait for Wayne Shelford to depart the scene. Shelford eventually did go, leaving Zinzan to fill out the All Black No 8 jersey.

Filling it out is exactly what he does. He has great upper body strength and is rumoured to hold a world record for shovelling shingle, no task for the physically delicate.

Zinzan's speed, power and determination to make it across the line, be it the advantage or the tryline, have been noticed across the Tasman.

Wally Lewis, he of the Brisbane Broncos and the unhappy scowl, picked Zinzan Brooke as the New Zealander most likely to become a league superstar, should he make the shift across the ditch.

According to press reports this almost happened. Graham Lowe's Manly club agreed with Lewis' assessment and are supposed to have had him signed on the dotted line for a maroon shirt with the Sea Eagles.

True or not, he stayed in the Auckland pack and in the Otago Ranfurly Shield challenge in September he slipped across for his 100th try in around 120 first-class matches.

Most discussions tend to revolve around the three Auckland players, Robin, Marty and Zinzan, but there are more of them. Two other Brookes are waiting just off stage.

Simon is the baby of the family. The 20-year-old is picked for bigger things. Brother Naera says of him: "He could be the best of the lot of us."

Naera himself is at the other end of the family. The oldest, at 30, he has a laid-back approach to rugby.

"I play an occasional game for Papatoetoe these days. But not many. A lot of weekends I head up to the farm and do the milking, which lets Mum and Dad come down to Auckland to see the games."

Mention of the Brooke's parents touches on the real key to their sporting success, especially mother Hine Brooke. She is a keen follower of the achievements of her sporting brood.

"Don't forget that not only were they always in the rugby reps but they were also terrific athletes," she reminds you. "I have got drawers and cupboards full of their certificates for things they won at track and field. I always thought both Marty and Robin were going to make a mark at athletics ahead of rugby. But rugby it turned out to be.

"They certainly kept me busy. I used to have dozens of pairs of socks and shorts to wash every Monday. They were all in the reps, under-14, under-16, under-18 as well as all their school and club games.

"I think there was about ten years of socks and jerseys."

To see the Brookes is to realise one thing. They are big, solid fellows. Did she have any trouble packing them in around the dining table?

"No, that was never something we had to worry about. We have this big twelve seater table, so no worries there."

It's the same thing with food. The family are farmers, first in Patumahoe and for over 20 years in the Warkworth district. Keeping the huge appetites of the family at bay was never too much of a problem.

"For a long time we could feed everyone off the farm — milk, jam, meat, everything," says Hine Brooke. "We used to have a pretty good garden in those days.

"In fact, when Naera was at school he was asked the price of a pint of milk and he didn't know. He had never had to buy any before."

Hine Brooke recalls the young Zinzan being fascinated with sheep.

"He used to be the keenest to do the shearing, mustering, crutching and anything to do with sheep. In the school holidays some of the boys would go off and work on shearing gangs.

"Zinzan was a very good shearer and he wasn't afraid of really hard work. I can give you one example of how good he was. One day, when he was only fourteen, he did three hundred sheep in a nine hour day of shearing."

That farm lifestyle played an important part in making the Brooke brothers such fine athletes.

THE Brooke family, home on the ranch. Back row: Zinzan, Simon, Robin, Naera, Martin. Front row: Margaret, Hine, Sandy.

Photo by : SRI MAIAVA-RUSDEN

"They would be playing rugby right through the winter. Then in the school holidays they wouldn't just sit around. They would be off on a nephew's shearing gang, as pressers or roustabouts."

These days the Warkworth farm is a lot quieter. The Brookes live in Auckland's Te Atatu, apart from Japan resident Marty and married sister Margaret.

Away from rugby the brothers are co-operating in a project to build each of them a house.

Naera explains: "At the moment we are building one for Zinzan. Then he will help out with the next one and so on, until everyone of us has got one."

Naera could not recall the Brookes ever being in the same rugby team. "But I think we might have all played in the same Gaelic football side. We are in the Roskill Rangers team."

Amongst the five boys is a sister, Margaret. She is second oldest, behind Naera and ahead of Martin, Zinzan, Robin and Simon in that order.

Hine Brooke remembers her daughter never had any trouble keeping five brothers under control. "They respected her. She was neither the boss nor the slave if I remember rightly. She was a badminton and netball player.

"Down at the badminton club they used to call her the 'babbling Brooke' although I don't think that's completely fair."

Naera's recollection is that: "She coped with us pretty well. I suppose she was one of us really, a funny shaped brother," he said with a laugh.

Denis Edwards is a freelance journalist who has been a regular contributor to *Rugby News* and several other prominent national publications in recent years.
He also edits the *Basketball Times*.

ZINZAN BROOKE in full cry for Auckland at Eden Park.   Photo by : PHOTOSPORT

A t the tender age of 25, Zinzan Brooke has managed what only three other New Zealand forwards have in the history of the game — he's scored 100 first-class tries.

Kel Tremain's record (for a forward) of 136 tries is well within the grasp of Brooke who has been averaging 20 tries a season since he broke into the first-class scene.

And winger Bernie Fraser's overall record of 171 tries may also come under threat.

Besides Tremain, the only other forwards to register a century of tries are Ian Kirkpatrick and Alan Sutherland.

Zinzan's hundredth try was hoisted in the Ranfurly Shield match against Otago during a particularly rosy patch in which he scored 10 tries in five outings for his union.

Incredibly, the dynamic No 8 has now scored 70 tries in 70 games for Auckland.

His first try, at first-class level, was scored for the Marist President's XV against the Condors in 1985 and his first try for Auckland came the next season.

Surprisingly he did not score any tries for Auckland in his first eight matches but a hat trick against Fiji in 1987 set a standard which he has maintained.

He has scored four tries in a match four times — for the All Blacks against Japan in 1987 and for Auckland against Taranaki in 1987, Wellington in 1989 and King Country in 1990.

He shares with Terry Wright the record for tries in Ranfurly Shield matches, a mark they've extended to 37. The old record of 30 was set by Hawkes Bay player Bert Grenside and had stood, until this season, for 64 years. ■

SUMMARY OF ZINZAN BROOKE'S TRYSCORING

	Games	Tries
Auckland	70	70
New Zealand	23	18
New Zealand Maoris	15	10
New Zealand Colts	8	1
Northern Zone Maoris	3	1
North Zone	4	1
New Zealand Trial	2	–
Barbarians	1	–
Marist President's XV	1	1
Totals	126	102

THE LEGEND OF BOB DEANS

By IAN BORTHWICK

Everyone knows the story of Bob Deans and the try he scored — or didn't score — at Cardiff on December 6, 1905. It has become one of rugby's greatest legends and recently one French journalist, recalling how the great-uncle of Robbie and Bruce swore with his dying breath that he scored it fair and square, said: "Over the years New Zealand's rugby has known of no more moving tale . . . "

But at Lancaster Park on May 28, 1988 there was an epilogue to the story. When Bruce Deans, the Canterbury shepherd, playing in his first test for New Zealand, scored against Wales in the 35th minute of play it seemed that after 83 years a great wrong had finally been put right. And that Deans' great-uncle Bob, who had died in 1908, could finally rest in peace.

The following is an extract from an article in the Paris daily *Liberation*. Published in July, 1988, it won Ian Borthwick the "XV d'Or 1988', a prize awarded each year for the best article on rugby in the French press.

"OUT here on the farm it's so calm and peaceful," says Bruce Deans the new All Black halfback.

"In any case, I know that when I come home after a match, the sheep won't give me a hard time, or tell me I was useless!"

One thing is sure — on his farm, David Kirk's successor in the No 9 jersey has all the peace and calm you could want.

The property, called "Kilmarnock", is about 110km north of Christchurch in the South Island of New Zealand. It's 870 hectares of hill country which Bruce works with his brother Robbie, the former All Black fullback who several years ago spent a season playing for Grenoble.

There are no other houses in sight, not even a village or settlement of any kind.

Except perhaps 35km away a lost village called Amberley . . . a few wooden houses planted on either side of the main road, a pub, a church — also of wood — and a few farm-suppliers' yards.

"At a certain point you will see some hills on the right," he says, explaining how to get there. "They are ours."

There they are, these hills, spotted with sheep, like a lawn covered with daisies. We are on the Canterbury Plain, at its northern-most end where the virtually-deserted road starts to climb over the Cheviot Hills. This plain has been settled for barely 150 years. But the pioneers have become farmers and the thousands upon thousands of sheep have helped bring wealth to the whole country. To such an extent that throughout the world the appellation "Canterbury" has become a reference, as much for the quality of its legs of lamb as for the rugby team of the same name.

Amongst the very first colonists to arrive in the province were the Deans. A name which would become one of the most prestigious in the growth of this colony and of its favourite sport, rugby football.

After another six kilometres of shingle road you come upon a few rough buildings and then the family home nestling behind the trees. Any doubt that this is in fact the Deans' place is quickly dispelled as there, just beside the dog kennels, is a clothesline with a collection of rugby jerseys of all sorts and colours hanging out to dry in the morning sun.

At Kilmarnock you are immediately struck by the sensation of total calm. One feels cut off from the world, surrounded by a heavy silence that is broken only by the singing of birds or the occasional barking of a sheepdog.

"I don't really notice it," smiles Bruce Deans. "Up here if I want to I can go for two weeks without seeing another soul.

I have never really felt the isolation and the solitude that other people talk to me about. After all, if I want to, I can just jump in the car and in ninety minutes I am in Christchurch.

THE LAST OF THE FARMERS

There was a time when New Zealand rugby was dominated by farmers, when the majority of the national team came from places just like Kilmarnock, each one more isolated than the rest. Kirkpatrick, Meads, Lochore, Clarke, Going, Mourie, Loveridge . . . they were all farmers. And who can forget the photo of the great Colin Meads training on his farm with a sheep under each arm?

Just as Welsh rugby comes from the valleys and the coalmines, so has New Zealand's rugby drawn its strength from the countryside.

But times change and the matches between Wales and New Zealand are no longer the traditional struggles between the miners and the farmers of the past.

Staff Jones is now the last of the miners in the Welsh team and in the current All Black team there is only Bruce Deans left as a representative of the rural world.

Bruce Deans the shepherd ("Don't write farmer, or sheep farmer or anything like that. I'm a shepherd and proud of it!" he insists) played his first test match at Christchurch on May 28, 1988.

On that day, out of the 10 tries scored by the All Blacks in beating Wales 52-3, the one the crowd applauded most was the one scored by Deans five minutes from halftime. For this was no normal touchdown. It warmed the hearts of Canterbury's people. Not simply because

BRUCE DEANS . . . seeking out the goalline, against Wales at Lancaster Park in 1988.　　　　Photo by : PETER BUSH

it was the first test try of one of their favourite sons but because when Deans dived over the goalline, the ball grasped firmly in both arms, it seemed that one of the great wrongs of rugby history had been set to right.

GREAT UNCLE BOB

The story goes back to 1905, when the first All Black team toured Great Britain. Amongst the players was a certain Bob Deans, the youngest member of the squad and the great-uncle of Bruce.

Some have called this team the greatest ever to visit the British Isles, setting new standards in the game and attaining levels of athleticism and physical fitness previously unheard of.

They played 33 matches in a row, scoring 868 points against only 47 for their opponents. There was only one defeat — that of the famous match against Wales in Cardiff. A match whose final score of 3–0 has become the most controversial result in the history of New Zealand rugby.

Thousands of words have already been written about this match and perhaps we will never know the true story. But the Deans incident is to this day still a talking point between Welsh and New Zealanders.

Briefly, the story is that the All Blacks claimed to score a try which the referee did not allow. Teddy Morgan scored a try for Wales just before halftime and Wales retained their 3–0 lead into the second half. But in the second half the All Blacks launched an attack. A superb break by Billy Wallace from within his own half . . . Wallace draws the defence and sends a long pass inside to Bob Deans. The young centre races away and despite the tackle of Rhys Gabe — or was it Teddy Morgan? — dives over the line to score.

At that moment the referee, dressed in street shoes and clothes, has been left far behind. When he finally arrives, Deans is no longer six inches over the line but six inches short. The Welsh swear that Gabe's tackle brought Deans down short of the line but the New Zealand forwards claim that before the referee could get there, the Welsh forwards had dragged Deans back by the heels.

"No try!" was Mr Dallas' decision but the All Blacks, and all New Zealand, have never forgiven this Welsh act of perfidy which had fooled the ref.

HE HAD TO SPEAK TO US BEFORE HE DIED

On his death bed scarcely three years later, Bob Deans swore once again that he had scored the try fair and square. Swept away at only 26 years of age by peritonitis he died much too early to see his great-nephew Bruce even things up with the Welsh. But he was not the only one who refused to take his secret to the grave . . .

Just as moving is the story of an old man who in 1983 managed to get a message to Bruce and Robbie Deans. It was the time when the Canterbury team was at the summit of its form and the Deans brothers were the darlings of the public.

Lying in hospital this old man, realising he had not much longer to live, asked to see the Deans boys.

"We went to see him, Robbie and I," remembers Bruce. "He said he absolutely had to speak to us before he died. All he said was this: He had been at the Cardiff match in 1905 and, with his own eyes, he had seen Uncle Bob score the try."

IT ALL HAPPENED IN SLOW MOTION

So it's hardly surprising that when Bruce knew he was selected for the first test against Wales the non-try seemed even more present.

"We have always lived with this story," he says. "Maybe we didn't talk about it every day but it's always been there, somewhere in my head. I thought that I wouldn't mind at all when my turn came, if I could score a try against Wales."

Justice, at least for the Deans, seems to have been done. And Bruce is not about to forget his "historic" try. In fact it is etched on his brain.

"The whole thing happened as if it were in slow motion. Even before I took the pass from John Gallagher I said to myself: 'Nothing can stop me now'. I dived over the line hanging on to the ball as hard as I could.

"It seemed to take ages before the referee blew his whistle. But when I heard it I thought: 'That's it! At last I've got it!' "

Four of his team mates, apparently aware of the symbolic importance of this try, rushed to congratulate him — something extremely rare for the All Blacks — and ran back with him to the halfway line.

"I can't say I was thinking exactly of Uncle Bob. But I said to myself: 'Those are four points which will go down in the score book and no one will ever be able to take them away from me'. " ■

NEW ZEALAND rugby's "originals", the trailblazing 1905 team which stumbled only once, against Wales. The man who claimed he scored a try that was never awarded, Bruce Deans' great uncle Bob Deans, is third from the left in the back row.

Ian Borthwick, who is based in Paris, is a freelance correspondent who contributes to rugby and political newspapers. The NZRFU appointed interpreter with the 1984 French touring team, he is the French correspondent for *Rugby News*.

RUGBY
THE INTERNATIONAL GAME
OR IS IT?

By GREG McGEE

You can picture the scene: A Wednesday afternoon provincial match in front of deserted terraces, between two teams who have no hope of winning the championship nor any fear of relegation.

A deadly dull and messy succession of scrums, lineouts and mauls which, if they roll anywhere, turn over on themselves and produce another put-in to another scrum.

Then — bingo! — one of the hookers gets himself sent off and the game changes. No more scrums, due to the danger of injury to someone playing out of position. Instead, the team which would have had the put-in has to take a tap penalty.

The game is instantly revitalised. Suddenly, there's the rare sight of players running at one another with the ball in hand, attempting to beat the defence with sleight of hand or of foot. Wonderful!

A veteran scribe was later moved to thank the ref for sending the hooker off and to apologise for enjoying the change so much, since it seemed to turn the game into something approaching — dare he admit it! — league.

That Wednesday afternoon encapsulated the real dangers of league to union — which have nothing to do with either professionalism or money.

Professionalism is already a non-issue. The attitude and commitment of the modern international player is already profoundly professional and the only remaining doubt is whether they'll ever get paid what they're worth.

And if that doesn't happen within a year or two, if players aren't at least realistically compensated, union will no longer have any pretensions to being a world game — it'll be a quaint backwater pastime like croquet, indulged in by upper class twits under the hegemony of an exclusive little Anglo-Saxon club which will no doubt still call itself the International Rugby Union. But there'll be precious little "international" about it.

The real issues for union are how to minimise the dead time in the game when the ball is not in play and how to maximise the time when the ball is in hand and being run at the opposition.

John Gallagher, when asked after his first game for Leeds what was the biggest difference between union and league, replied that in union he had to play for only 25 minutes out of every 80, whereas in league he had to play for over 70 minutes out of every 80.

That extra 45 minutes has to add up to a heck of a lot more entertainment value for every dollar spent by the spectator!

And whatever the union connoisseur's pleasure in the high arts of scrummaging, mauls, rucks and lineouts, a player running with the ball in hand remains both the purest expression of rugby and the most attractive, entertaining and accessible part of the game for the average spectator.

So how does union approach these challenges? Can anything be learned from league which has already been there and done that?

In an attempt to appeal to the masses, league has eliminated flankers, eliminated the lineout, eliminated second phase play (rucks and mauls) as a means of gaining or losing possession, emasculated the scrum so that it is nothing more than a means of restarting the game and forced each team to hand over possession after six plays.

These measures haven't proven to be the complete answer. The 1989 Aussie grand final between Canberra and Balmain was superb entertainment but — despite the hoopla — anyone who subscribed to Sky in 1990 in the hope of seeing that sort of spectacle week after week would have to be deeply disappointed.

League's six plays can be even more boring than the most pedestrian game of union: the props from Team A take it up the middle twice and get crunched; a second rower takes it up once a bit wider and gets crunched; they move it to the backs twice and they get crunched; and if Team A still has the pill after all this there's a huge hack downfield by someone who has the kicking skills of an ox.

Then the same process is repeated by Team B — and can be repeated ad infinitum, if no one makes a defensive error or shows some attacking genius.

It can be about as exciting as watching lowest common denominator television which is also formulaically designed to appeal to people who don't have to exercise any critical faculties while watching. And which is also, very often, excruciatingly repetitive in its rhythms.

Union is a far more complex game and there are several precious elements which flow from that complexity.

Union players, for instance, have to have a wider range of skills, generally, and there are a wider range of specialist positions which require a wider range of body types.

This is increasingly unique in the various forms of "footy" throughout the world — American football and league and soccer all put a premium on particular body types.

In league and gridiron, you won't see the 2m (6ft 6in) Ian Jones beanpole. In soccer, you won't see a Richard Loe — a cause of relief for goalkeepers!

In gridiron, neither a Loe nor a Grant Fox would ever get the ball in hand. Loe would be reduced to a series of ritualised head-butts and Fox would be wheeled out to kick a ball which he wouldn't even hold to place.

When the French say all the world can play rugby, they aren't talking about the United Nations so much as Fatty and Skinny, Lofty and Shorty and everyone in between.

Union also has more pretensions to being a truly international game than league.

Last year, in Italy, my mate on the Italian Federation was working mightily towards Italy's big qualifying play-off this year with Romania, Spain and (I think) Holland.

Spain beat the likes of Poland and Belgium in order to qualify for this play-off, while the Dutch beat Portugal and Sweden.

The Soviet Union this year toured Australia; and countries as diverse as Japan, Argentina and Canada all have credible teams and aspirations towards a World Cup which is worthy of the name.

League's World Cup is by contrast only slightly more international than a baseball "World Series". Very few countries have credible international teams, despite the Aussie league's rather desperate attempts to export it to the far-flung edges of civilisation like Western Australia, Victoria and the United States.

This doesn't mean, however, that union should be complacent. If union isn't prepared to adapt and become more entertaining, league will continue to make inroads on the discretionary and sponsorship dollar.

One of union's most precious elements is also its achilles heel — the continuity between primary and secondary phase play. At its best — read Auckland of the '80s, France pre-Fouroux and the All Blacks pre-1990 — this continuity can be

JOHN GALLAGHER . . . rugby player.   Photo by : RUSSELL CHEYNE, Allsport

exhilarating. It puts a premium on the mobility and agility of even the largest players.

But secondary play can also be static — the five minute maul! — and boring and messy, with constant infringements of the very complex rules governing the behaviour of players in those split-seconds at the interface of primary and secondary phase.

Too often, the result is that far from leading to continuity of play, it ends up with more static primary phase set plays — scrums, in other words, or kicks to touch leading to lineouts.

League's answer to this problem was to simply eliminate second phase play altogether. If the ballcarrier is tackled and cannot offload before he's securely held, play must stop while the tackled player gets up and plays the ball back with his heel.

But this solution removes all complexity from league and for my money makes it even more predictable and formulaic.

Is there a middle ground for union? A solution or a series of changes which would keep the ball in play longer and simplify the transition between primary and secondary phases with the objective of ensuring continuity of play?

This area of union, the interface between primary and secondary phase play, has been fiddled with by the lawmakers for many many years. Sometimes the rules are fine-tuned to facilitate rucks and sometimes, as recently, to encourage mauls.

The changes seem to be motivated by safety and aesthetic concerns — though New Zealand sceptics would say that the laws seem to be changed as soon as the All Blacks prove masters of the last set of changes. If that's so, expect some more fiddling to curb the rolling maul!

We now have very complex rules governing actions which happen in a timeframe of split-seconds. This nexus of rules, allied to the split-second timeframes, mean that players constantly infringe the rules and that referees have to react too quickly to enforce them properly.

Sometimes the best policy in situations like this is to step back and look at what would happen if that nexus of rules were removed altogether. And then to look at the history of those rules — what was the first rule in this area? What was the

reason for it? Why was it amended?

Union desperately needs a man or woman of vision to walk backwards through this particular jungle to the mangroves wherein secondary phase play was first conceived.

Once there, with his feet in the bog, this latter-day pioneer should fix his eyes on the sunlit slopes where the perfect game of rugby is played, where the continuity between first and second phase play is as fluid and smooth as fine wine and where the ball is in play 79 minutes 59 seconds out of every 80 minutes. And then he should work out how to get there. In one foul swoop, preferably.

There should be no delusions about the magnitude of the task — Orville and Wilbur Wright didn't have to take off from a bog and fly to a plateau.

But if union could clean up that nexus and achieve greater continuity between the two phases of play, it would have nothing further to fear from league.

Indeed, 20 years down the track, the only problem might be how to assimilate the paupers of league into a fully professional union which would have already taken the US by storm and would be rapidly taking on soccer's mantle as The World Game. ■

JOHN GALLAGHER . . . league player.   Photo by : MIKE BRETT, UK

Greg McGee is a writer for theatre (*Foreskins Lament* and *Out In The Cold*) and television (*Roche and Erebus : The Aftermath*) and a rugby nut. Back in the early 1970s he represented New Zealand Juniors and was close to All Black selection.

DID YOU KNOW?

By JOHN SINCLAIR

That in 1888–89 Great Britain was toured by the strangest rugby touring side the world has ever seen.

And it was a world first, being the first time the home country had been toured by any overseas rugby side, from any country, let alone a self-styled New Zealand Maori team.

The "Natives" played 108 games on a world trip that lasted 14 months.

Usually averaging three games a week, they played 74 games in Britain in six months.

They were mocked as being not much better than a social side because of mates rates and nepotism in selection (nearly one third of the team came from two families . . . there were three Wynyard brothers and five Warbricks).

Despite predictions like the Otago Rugby Union's "they won't win a single game" and the Hawkes Bay journalist's "they couldn't beat English schoolboys", they won 70 per cent of their games . . . in a punishing games schedule that today's match secretaries would nightmare over.

The team started out as the Maoris, but short in four positions before departure press-ganged four ring-in Pakehas.

No longer the Maoris, they switched their name to the Native team.

Joe Warbrick was captain of the 1888–89 Native team. He was one of the greatest players of his era, a great dropkick exponent.

On tour of Australia with the 1884 New Zealand team he rocked the locals with his casual all-you-have-to-do-is-take-aim style when putting pots over from near halfway.

He played fullback for Auckland against Otago, aged 15.

Unfortunately Joe got crocked just before the tour and a first game aggravation virtually rendered him deck cargo from then on.

No rugby international ever suffered a more heroic or bizarre death.

In 1903, seeing two English women standing perilously close to the about to erupt Waimungu Geyser . . . knowing the odds stacked against him . . . he gambled on getting to them in time. All three lost.

The Native team's schedule for November 1888 was . . . playing on the 3rd, 5th, 7th, 10th, 12th, 14th, 17th, 20th, 22nd, 23rd, 24th (that's three days on end), 26th, 28th then over to beat Ireland 13–4 in the first ever rugby international.

Even World Cup winning All Blacks would run for cover from those dates.

No team before or since has ever played with such heart and soul and fire in the belly. Linament was bought by the bottle. Then by the case.

With so many legitimate claims for sprained ankles, dislocated shoulders and injured limbs, the insurance company exercised an escape clause and backed off. The Maoris had to play from sick beds.

Having 'flu was no excuse. Forwards had to play as backs and vice versa.

Often players couldn't go in hard for tackles in case they worsened the injury they already had and there were no replacements.

On one occasion four players were crocked and a team of 11 had to soldier on.

But at least they had started that day with a full team. Another time only 14 men took the field.

They rarely had more than a dozen completely fit players. One seeming malingerer was told to get stuck in. He did. He had TB and died shortly after returning to New Zealand.

Two of the players finished up in mental homes.

THE amazing 1888 Native team. They played 108 games on a world trip that lasted 14 months.

Ice and snow playing conditions were something Polynesians hadn't even read about. At one game the opposition were so cold and numb they couldn't continue.

But the Maori backline had the improvised answer for that . . . when they were shivering cold once and presumably their own forwards controlled the game, the Maori backline wore overcoats.

One or two of the Maoris weren't at all comfortable playing in boots. With only one set of playing gear, frequently still wet or damp, they sometimes turned out in composite attire. Part football gear, part street clothing.

All touring sides suffer strange decisions. Mind you, the Natives asked for some of it. Those in the UK weren't accustomed to colonials' inherent suspicion of unchallenged authority and British refs were backchatted too much.

It has been said that if the 10 yard rule had applied then the Natives would have played all their games in their own dead ball area.

But in one important game they ran up against a real hometowner.

He was never off their backs and when a British player tore his strides, play stopped.

The Maoris were part of the courteous screen.

An opposing player picked up the dead ball, dotted down for a try and had it allowed.

That did it three of the Maoris said, well stuff it, and walked off the field. It took some placating to get them to resume play later!

That it was so cold when the All Blacks played the British Lions at Dunedin's Carisbrook in 1983 that many of the New Zealanders took the field wearing wet suits under their jerseys.

Allan Hewson, Stu Wilson and Steven Pokere donned mittens and Bernie Fraser wrapped his feet in plastic before pulling on his boots.

It was so cold that 16-stone props like John Ashworth were shivering uncontrollably when they returned to the dressing room — after 80 minutes of physical contact in scrums and rucks and lineouts.

Throughout the Friday rain, hail, sleet and occasionally light snow fell in Dunedin, accompanied by a biting southerly. Hail showers fell intermittently during the test.

The Lions' famous flyhalf Ollie Campbell described the conditions as the worst in his experience.

"After five minutes I had no feeling in my hands or my feet and you can't play football properly like that," he said.

The All Blacks won the game 15–8.

Generally, a prestigious rugby club is formed after long and careful planning. Barbarians started at a riproaring grog and oyster boozeroo.

A rugby club name is usually carefully selected with a special significance.

Barbarians cannot remember who thought up their name, or whether it has significance to anything, let alone rugby.

Normally, you start a rugby club in a hardcore rugby area. Barbarians started in Bradford, home of league football.

Most rugby clubs urge players on to win almost at all costs. That attitude is frowned on in Barbarians, by the "alickadoos" — the good natured reference to Golden Oldies when "all-they-can-do" is give advice.

Most rugby clubs have selectors who pick and advise players. Barbarians have members who scout for likely players but selection is made by the secretary who doesn't watch games.

Outside of Britain it was neither South Africa (1889) nor New Zealand (1892) which was the first country to form a Rugby Football Union.

It was Australia in 1875 — only a couple of years after England (1871), Scotland (1873) Ireland (1879) and Wales (1880).

Rugby league was started in Australia by a New Zealander in 1908 — by a Wellingtonian who wanted to cash in on the extraordinary gate takings of the 1905 Originals in the UK.

So he suggested to the British league controllers that he bring cash players on tour in 1907.

He quickly signed up four of the 1905 Originals to go back again . . . they were George Smith, Duncan McGregor, Billy Mackrell and Massa Johnson, as well as a skim of top New Zealand provincial players.

It was on their way back from the UK that they played games in Australia. It was said at the time that the lure of the cash game spread like rabbits.

Which later often produced the story of the outback farmer who said: "What

I'd give to grab the bloke who introduced the first rabbit to Australia." The reply he got was: "The bloke I'd like to lay my hands on was the one who brought the second rabbit."

In a country district in Taranaki a boastful club player was always drawing team mates' attention to his own skill.

In one game, he really did put up a class drop kick from near halfway. The sideline applause wasn't enough . . . and he called to a player: "Well how about that . . . wasn't it a beaut?"

The reply he got was: "Yeah, it was. What a pity the club can't have it stuffed!"

The 1924 Invincibles were the only team this century to make a major tour and *win* every game. In 1891 a British rugby team toured South Africa . . . played 20, won 20.

While the 1924 All Blacks had a triumphant tour of the Old Country, the 1924 Lions had their worst ever overseas tour . . . winning only nine of 21 games, on tour in South Africa.

What positions did South African rugby chief Danie Craven play in test matches? Most people remember him as a halfback but he also played internationals at first-five, centre and No 8.

Billy Wallace, 1903–08 All Black, was one of New Zealand's most versatile players. He occasionally played halfback but was usually at first-five or second-five in club rugby, while for provincial matches or internationals he was either on the wing or at fullback.

Yet neither had anything on Welsh player Arthur Harding.

He played halfback against the Original Springboks and was a front row and back row forward against the Original All Blacks and Original Wallabies.

He toured New Zealand with the 1904 British team, captained the Anglo-Welsh side back to New Zealand in 1908, then immigrated here in 1910.

He turned out twice for Wanganui — once as fullback, the other time as wing forward!

The Calcutta Cup has always been associated with the England-Scotland games. In 1873, ardent rugger fans in India formed the Calcutta Football Club.

The unrugby clique finally saw its demise ... so they drew their funds out of the bank, in rupees, and had the coins melted down and fashioned into an 18in high typical Indian bazaar ornament.

Highly prized for its traditional value, it is annually on display in a security minded jewellers display window prior to the game itself, after which it is handed around the players as a loving Cup then hidden away in bank vaults.

One year on display, it caught the eye of a London property tycoon. Not interested in rugby he couldn't accept that it was simply not for sale at any price.

Being told its value he doubled it ... and finally went as high as 40 times its valuation. Still not for sale.

He stormed out of the shop. He was on his way as patron of a boys scout camp and wanted something as a prize at their tenting competition.

South Africa's inter-provincial Currie Cup was donated by Sir Donald Currie, head of the Castle Line. He originally gave it to the South African side which did the best against the touring 1891 British visitors. The province in time passed it over to the South African Rugby Board,

When the Original All Blacks, Original Springboks and Original Wallabies all toured the UK they had games refereed by the top Welsh referee Gil Evans.

He in turn gave the whistle to the top Welsh referee of a later decade, Albert Freethy.

Freethy used it to referee the rugby final at the 1924 Olympics in Paris the last time rugby was in the Olympics (USA beat France 17–3).

Freethy also used it to send Cyril Brownlie off at Twickenham in 1925.

In 1969, Stan Dean presented it to the Rugby Museum.

In 1987, it started the first Rugby World Cup.

Also used too at the start of the World Cup was the coin used in the toss at the 1925 England–New Zealand test.

The coin, as a souvenir value, later had a rose embossed on one side and a fernleaf on the other.

WET SUITS were worn by many of the All Blacks to help them survive the cold against the British Lions in Dunedin in 1983. Looking pleased as punch after their 15–8 victory are: Back row — Wayne Smith, Bernie Fraser, Robbie Deans (reserve), Allan Hewson, Stu Wilson, Arthur Stone. Front row — Dave Loveridge, Warwick Taylor, Steven Pokere.

Photo by : PETER BUSH

Australian referee Bob Fordham confirmed that the game call for the toss was not heads or tails but "rose or fernleaf".

On tour in 1951–52 a bitter game developed between the touring Springboks and a country side in England.

South African captain Basil Kenyon called out in English: "Now settle down, settle down . . . cut out all this fighting . . . "

Then, in Afrikaans, he added: "I'll give you five minutes to sort those bastards out, then get on with the game!"

It was on this tour in 1951–52 that Hennie Muller had a group at a country mansion. As they sat to dinner, Hennie was asked to say grace.

He respectfully hung his head and intoned in Afrikaans: "I'll thump anyone I catch trying to souvenir His Lordship's crested silver . . . amen."

How did the Lions get their colours? On the 1930 voyage out to New Zealand the five Irish members of the touring party pointed out that the red, white and blue was all very well but what recognition were they getting.

So the team amongst themselves devised the idea of adding a green flash to their stockings.

The great Maori fullback George Nepia toured with the 1924 Invincibles, playing in every game, the only time it has ever been done on a major tour.

George gave long service to the game . . . having been capped as a New Zealand player while still a teenager.

His rugby career began as a winger, then as a midfield back.

Still playing first-class games when over 40, he scored his most memorable try taking part in a charity game in his early fifties.

The ball came straight towards him from a miskicked clearance . . . he caught it . . . all those unrequited midfield instincts welled up in him. He saw the gap . . . sidestepped and fended, to touch down under the posts.

A unique try, to a standing ovation. What made it unique was he was referee at the time.

GEORGE NEPIA . . . *played in every match on the 1924 All Blacks' tour of the UK and France. They won the lot.*

Before making the tour in 1905 New Zealand asked for some guarantees to cover their expenses which they got everywhere except Scotland.

Mindful that they had lost money on a Canadian rugby visit the year before and listening to Darkie Bedell-Sivright (captain of the 1904 British team to Australasia) who said the New Zealanders wouldn't be up to much . . . Scotland opted to put the risk on us.

But by the time the All Blacks got to Scotland they were sporting magnets. Extra trains were put on to most games.

Passengers were allowed to sleep in trains . . . accommodation everywhere booked out. (In Wales miners from the Valleys walked 20 miles to get to a game and walked back later.)

Realising they had underestimated the tourists, the Scots seemed to go out of their way to be ornery, to downgrade the match.

They wouldn't class it an international . . . wouldn't award caps.

It was the only venue where New Zealand wasn't welcomed at the railway station by union officials.

Groundsmen "forgot" to put straw down and after a hard frost the Scots wanted the game abandoned. The crowd didn't. Then they argued the toss on length of halves.

Said New Zealand would have to provide the ball. We didn't have one. They produced an old one that looked as if it had been mated with a cucumber. Their attitude seemed to infect others. When the boys put their boots out to be cleaned at the hotel they found them filled with breadcrumbs.

The Scots actually played very well (Dave Gallaher later said New Zealand was markedly inferior to Scottish and Irish forwards with the ball at toe). Scottish breaches appeared to be overlooked by the ref . . . but four New Zealand likely tries were recalled for marginal forward passes. The Scots in the lead kicked the ball up into the stand to use up time.

In a hard game that could have gone either way . . . Scottish writers inferred the better team lost . . . English papers that the better team finally won.

It was the only place where the team got no entertainment laid on by rugby followers. All their hospitality came from a soccer club which "adopted" them and gave them full use of their club facilities.

Finding them sitting around doing nothing they set up a greatly appreciated musical evening. It was the soccer people who saw them off on the train.

It all contrasted so sharply with the next stopover — Ireland — where waiting crowds broke down railings and police barriers to cheer the All Blacks at the station on arrival.

The '24 team beat Scotland 12–7.

John Sinclair, based in Palmerston North, is the founder of New Zealand's national rugby museum there. He also pioneered rugby supporters overseas tours.

BEEGEE
– THE WONDER WINGER

By BOB HOWITT

Long after the final whistle to Auckland and New Zealand matches you usually found Bryan Williams surrounded by hundreds of youngsters, happily signing autographs.

And those lucky enough to get to after-match functions or to share Beegee's company in any capacity never ceased to be impressed with the man's modesty and humility.

Astonishing, really, when you consider that he had probably just scored the try of the season, or banged over a 60-metre penalty goal or crash-tackled some hapless opponent into the dust.

Being natural and co-operative didn't require any special effort from Bryan Williams, the most exciting back uncovered in New Zealand rugby since Ron Jarden.

His personality was shaped very strongly by his own experiences in rugby.

When he travelled to Eden Park by bus for a representative or international match as a player, he reflected upon the days when he would walk three miles to Eden Park and three miles home to see Ranfurly Shield matches.

"The first shield match I went to was when Waka Nathan scored behind the posts in the last minute to beat Canterbury," recalls Williams.

"I was one of the forty thousand yelling themselves hoarse as he ran round behind the posts.

"That match really hooked me and I never missed another shield match during Auckland's golden era."

Bryan's mum used to give him a shilling for the bus fare, but he was quick to realise that by walking the six miles involved he could spend the money on a bag of chips!

Young Bryan bought a programme every visit and the full set of shield programmes are among his most prized possessions today.

After he exploded on to the All Black scene in 1970 there were few setbacks for "Beegee". But when they did come he took them as calmly and naturally as he did his successes which were substantially greater.

Again, he reflected upon incidents in his youth.

When he was 11 he won his way into the Auckland primary schools representative team.

The following year he considered himself a certainty for selection again.

"Because I was so cock-sure I'd made the team I didn't train half as hard and my form dropped.

"When the team was announced at Eden Park my name wasn't there. It was the most traumatic thing that had happened in my life till then.

"I walked the three miles home in the rain, crying all the way!

"It was a salutory lesson — one I've never forgotten."

An All Black till he was 28, Williams made a staggering contribution to New Zealand rugby.

He became the greatest tryscorer in All Black history. His total of 66 took him past the record of James Hunter's which had survived since 1907. Hunter aggregated 49 tries and Ian Kirkpatrick went on to score 50.

With the points he accrued as part-time goalkicker, also, Beegee finished third highest All Black pointscorer of all time, behind only the legendary Don Clarke and Fergie McCormick and ahead of such free scorers as Billy Wallace, Mark Nicholls, Bob Scott and Ron Jarden.

The first time Bryan Williams pulled on a football jersey it was to play league.

"My brothers Ces and Ken were rugby-mad and I took a fair ribbing when I announced I was going to play league.

"It was only because all my mates joined the Ponsonby league club, and I tagged along with them. If my brothers ribbed me, my parents stood up for me."

It's intriguing to reflect that Bryan Williams who, during his international career, received some giant league offers — the biggest was $24,000 to join Wigan — was twice "let go" by league.

The first time was when he was 11.

He'd played league from when he was five and would have kept going but suddenly there was no team for him.

"My side had disbanded. So my brothers seized on the opportunity and got me into the Ponsonby rugby twelfth grade team."

The next occasion was when he was 14 and in his second year at Mt Albert Grammar School.

"My friends put pressure on me and I was easily influenced because there was a New Zealand schoolboys league team going to Australia at the end of the year.

"I played rugby for the Mt Albert three B team in the morning and league for Marist in the afternoons.

"It was a good team and I was chosen for the Auckland under-fifteen side, made reserve for North Island and went into the trials for the New Zealand team.

"I felt I'd done enough to be selected, but when the team for Australia was announced my name was missing.

"I vowed and declared I would never play league again.

"Dave Sorenson was in the same situation as me. We've since been reliably informed that we were left out because we had played rugby the year before."

What code might Bryan have concentrated on had he been selected to tour Australia then?

"I've often reflected on that myself. Who knows?"

Williams had his first taste of representative rugby when he was chosen for the Auckland Roller Mills team in 1961, age 11.

"We stayed on a farm at Waiuku — it was a wonderful experience.

"I got into the team only after a harsh series of trials. It was my first experience of learning to accept success and failure. Some kids were so disappointed at missing the team they cried."

What Williams describes as an "exhilarating" experience in the Roller Mills team made rugby "everything" to him after that.

"I dreamed about rugby, made sure of seeing every big match at Eden Park and read everything I could on the game."

"Beegee" had five years at Mt Albert Grammar.

His rugby started in the 4A (under nine stone) team.

"Boy, it was tough. There was no age limit. It was one of the hardest years of my career. I was young and not physically hardened."

In 1964, the year he made his bid for the New Zealand league team, he played for the 3Bs with moderate success.

The following year he was selected for the first XV and came under coach Eugene Cheraton — "Cherry" as he was popularly known.

"His training was murderous. I've never trained harder since.

"We had these grassy slopes at Mt Albert. He used to make us piggy-back fellow players up there; other times we'd sprint up the slope and make a tackle at the summit.

"He even made you lie on your back and got players, in boots, to walk up and down you.

"His idea of an 'easy day' was to run two or three times up Mt Albert itself."

Super-fit Williams played second-five and recalls that he tried to break every time he got the ball.

"I was only a fourteen-year-old against seventeen-year-olds and my tactics finally led to a busted shoulder."

In 1966 an Auckland secondary schools team toured Australia but Williams was out of consideration because of a recurring groin injury.

Things perked up in 1967, his fifth and final year at MAGS.

After taking out the sprint, long jump, discus and shot titles during the summer,

BRYAN WILLIAMS in full cry during his second tour of South Africa in 1976.   Photo by : WESSEL OOSTHUIZEN

he became first-five and vice captain of the first XV (skip was Bernie Allen who has since represented Auckland as a prop).

"I kicked and ran a lot that year, and thoroughly enjoyed it. As a winger now I appreciate what it is to handle the ball, and get pretty annoyed on the wing at times when I'm neglected."

Williams that year made the Auckland secondary schools team, captained by Laurie Knight.

"After we'd beaten New South Wales and drawn with Fiji we went down to Waikato, very complacent, and got stuffed.

"That was another important lesson!"

During 1967, at the tender age of 16, "Beegee" made his senior debut. It happened during the school holidays.

"Malcolm Dick, Ponsonby's champion winger, was away at the All Black trials and my brothers Ces and Ken both said to bring my gear because the team was short.

"I'm sure it was all a jack-up, because when I got to Eden Park they told me Trevor Paterson wasn't there and I would have to play.

"I played on the wing and scored a try, which, as you can guess, made a mighty big impression on me."

To score the try Williams had to side-step the Manukau fullback Roger Whatman, a feat which hinted at the exciting things to come from young Williams.

During the next summer the Ponsonby seniors worked furiously to raise enough finance to undertake a trip to Japan. There was never any suggestion young Bryan should go.

Then, three weeks before take-off, Malcolm Dick withdrew for business reasons and "Beegee" was asked to join the team.

"That was a lucky break. I hadn't help raise any of the money, but suddenly I was going with 'em."

Williams played in every match on tour, finishing with 10 tries. Malcolm Dick couldn't have done better. The Ponsonby players were already beginning to see in young Williams another All Black.

Williams himself recalls with amusement the first two matches.

"Before the games there they always take a composite photo, all the players in.

"Before the first match all the Japanese players were grim-faced, the Ponsonby guys casual.

"We lost that first match thirty to seven. In the second group photo, the Ponsonby players were even more serious looking than the Japanese!"

Back home, with Malcolm Dick available and brother Ken (an Auckland rep and 1968 All Black trialist) in top form, Bryan was no sitter for a place in the Ponsonby team. Coach Eric Boggs nursed him along, playing him only when he thought Williams needed a game.

Williams' occasional appearances for Ponsonby were sufficient for him to be named in the Auckland Colts team for the East Coast tour.

He marked his representative debut with four tries and two conversions against East Coast at Ruatoria and scored another try in his next match against Poverty Bay.

He was now being branded the "find" of the year, a footballer with a big future.

Because he turned out for the senior reserves when Eric Boggs didn't want him, he qualified for the reserves' end-of-season trip to Noumea.

In 1969 Bob Graham made Williams a regular in the Auckland team.

"I should have been on the wing, but Grahame Thorne had a dust-up with Bob Graham and dropped out for a while. When he returned I was centre and Thorney went on to the wing.

"We never did rate each other too highly as centres. Grahame was a brilliant individual. To play outside each other was not exactly a dream ride!"

Williams came close to national recognition but in the New Zealand Juniors trials at Athletic Park Williams and Howard Joseph crash-tackled each other out of the match.

"We did such a great job on each other, the selectors brought Mick Duncan in from the wing for the Juniors' match against Tonga!"

Aucklanders who had witnessed Williams' genius at club and rep level were certain by the time 1970 came round that he was an All Black. But the selectors needed convincing.

Williams' own clubmate Malcolm Dick helped solve that problem.

"He was instrumental in getting me into several important pre-season matches where I did okay."

Williams had a so-so trial at Palmerston North and got almost no attacking opportunities in the final trial at Athletic Park.

But he did tear off a series of magnificent tackles. He twice caught Bruce Hunter from behind and once got across in cover defence to bowl Mick O'Callaghan into touch.

Williams and Hunter made the team to South Africa but O'Callaghan — whom Williams rates as the unlucky winger of the trials — missed out.

That was in May. By the end of August Bryan Williams, 18, was being heralded as the greatest winger in the world. South Africans loved him. He was to receive more than 1500 fan letters from South Africa.

And yet Williams considered he was lucky to succeed.

"Certainly lucky at the start. Before the tour a groin injury troubled me and I started the tour with my leg bandaged."

Williams didn't play in Perth on the way across. Hunter had to play twice in the one afternoon to make up the numbers.

"Before my first game in South Africa, at Bethlehem, we played a game of touch rugby. Fergie McCormick caught me from behind. I was terribly embarrassed — I was supposed to be a winger. I felt I wasn't fast enough and wondered what I was in for.

"Luckily, because the opposition at Bethlehem was so weak I scored two tries and boosted my confidence.

"If the opposition had been tough, who knows what may have happened."

Williams soon established himself in the top line-up and he and fellow Ponsonby man Malcolm Dick were the first test wingers. Williams scored New Zealand's only try — set up for him by Sid Going who had replaced Chris Laidlaw — in the 17-6 loss.

"We were stunned by the ferocity of South Africa's attack in that first test. I've never experienced such a fanatical approach since. We may have been complacent, but I felt the Springboks' ferocity that day would have pushed aside anything."

Williams should have had a try in the second test, too, but the referee allowed himself to be over-ruled by touch judge Max Baise.

"I scored, clear enough. There was no doubt about it. I'd started to cut back infield and went over the line in a tackle, landing on my back and forcing the ball as I did so. My tackler carried on over the top of me and took out the corner flag. The ref, after saying it was a try, let himself get talked out of it. Instead of a clear-cut win, it forced Fergie McCormick into an agonising last-minute penalty kick to give us the test nine points to eight."

Between the second and third tests Williams enjoyed what he describes as "the great week".

He scored two tries against Western Province at Newlands and three more against South African Country at East London, kicking five goals as well.

"Everything went right for me. Twice the ball bounced straight into my hands with players all around me."

Williams kicked a penalty goal for New Zealand's only points in the dismal third test loss and then ran in a fabulous try (once more created by Sid Going) in the final test at Ellis Park. Not content with getting across the goalline Williams — in almost contemptuous mood — sidestepped three Springboks in the in-goal area before dotting down behind the posts.

Williams regards his second try against Eastern Province on that tour as his "greatest ever".

"Funnily enough I actually dropped the pass to me. I backheeled the ball and just took off — scoring about eighty yards upfield."

Williams finished the tour with 14 tries and six goals for 56 points.

Sackloads of mail, from admiring fans, followed him home.

He set out to answer every letter, with assistance from his mum, but finally gave up when the fan mail went over the thousand mark.

One admirer, a 26-year-old coloured girl from Cape Town, visited New Zealand in 1974, and was entertained by Bryan and his mother.

Malcolm Dick announced his retirement after the tour and said in an interview that Bryan Williams' toughest times lay ahead, that now he had become famous everyone would be "agin him".

"Never a truer word was spoken. Where previously I'd faced one opponent per match, now I faced two or three."

Williams failed to reproduce in New Zealand in 1971 the form that had dazzled South African fans.

"Before 1970 I went on a lot of road runs. When I came to a hill I'd say 'get to the top and you'll go to South Africa'. In 1971 I'd get halfway up the hill and say 'that's okay'. "

Williams paid the penalty for an incomplete preparation and was plagued by injury throughout 1971.

He looked philosophically at the 2½–1½ loss to the Lions.

"In South Africa I was the baby of the team. Suddenly, one year later I was the most experienced player in the backline after Sid Going and Wayne Cottrell. We had new forwards too — Peter Whiting, Tane Norton, Alan McNaughton and Richie Guy.

"We had seven new caps in the first test. In the circumstances I reckon we did okay."

Williams was used at centre in the first test, lost 9–3.

"I beat John Dawes a few times — I felt he was their weak point — but Mike Gibson got me each time in cover defence."

Williams was awarded a penalty try in the second test when Gerald Davies wrapped him up before he could secure Sid Going's pass near the goalline.

He missed the third test with injury and saw little of the action in the drawn fourth test at Eden Park.

Despite his leg injuries, Williams scored 12 tries for Auckland while his goalkicking helped lift the Ranfurly Shield from Canterbury. "Beegee" landed three superb 45-yarders in Auckland's thrilling 20–16 win.

If Williams was encouraged on the internal tour in 1972, when coach Jack Gleeson devised special moves just to get the ball to him (he responded with 12 tries from nine appearances) he experienced extreme frustration later in the year when the seventh All Blacks went to Britain and France.

In 25 matches he scored only seven tries. He became neglected on the wing and went into a state of virtual revolt.

"Perhaps I didn't try hard enough. I didn't go looking for work. Grant Batty was on his first tour and full of enthusiasm and did look for work. He scored twenty-one tries and I scored seven."

Williams finds it hard to discuss that tour which he regards as a low point in his career.

He does admit that the placing of Llanelli and Cardiff in the first week, with the subsequent results (a loss at Llanelli and a glorious punch-up against Cardiff) had a profound impact on the whole tour.

Back home he felt it unfair that the All Blacks, who had battled through three seasons in a row, should be asked to undertake an internal tour.

"I found my examinations a convenient excuse to miss the internal tour."

Beegee was swotting hard when the All Blacks went down to the Juniors and the Presidents XV before pulling themselves together.

In 1974 Williams felt he had to re-establish himself.

It didn't shape up that way when he suffered a thigh injury playing for the All Blacks against Western Australia in Perth.

He was sidelined for two-and-a-half weeks and then gave probably his worst-ever All Black display, against New South Wales.

Owen Stephens left him for dead once and "Beegee" had no pace or, seemingly, enthusiasm.

"I was still worried about my thigh and when I was kicked on the leg it seized up. I should have come off, but I thought I would see out the match."

In those days the All Blacks travelled overseas without their own physiotherapist, and as Beegee was referred from one medical canthority to another, he became progressively more depressed.

But the New South Wales match got him back into action and from that point his form improved rapidly, allowing him to contribute significantly to the series win over the Aussies.

After helping Auckland win the Ranfurly Shield, in a runaway against Wellington, Williams hit heights on the Irish tour that had Fleet Street journalists running out of adjectives.

Williams scored three tries in Ireland and in each instance he had to motor through, over or around resolute opponents to get to the goalline. And his defence was equally dynamic.

He made JJ Williams — top tryscorer on the Lions' triumphant tour of South Africa — look positively second-rate at Cardiff Arms Park and, for the first time, outplayed Gerald Davies, inspiring more than one British journalist to brand him the best winger in the world.

The 1975 season was a big one for Williams, although modest for the All Blacks, who took the field only once — on a flooded Eden Park against Scotland. Beegee wowed the sodden fans with two glorious tries in the remarkable 24–0 victory.

Beegee had earlier revisited South Africa with his club Ponsonby and went on to help Auckland survive seven challenges for the Ranfurly Shield.

And it was off to South Africa again the following year, in a likely-looking All Black team managed by Noel Stanley, coached by JJ Stewart and captained by Andy Leslie.

There were early delights for Beegee, three tries in the tour opener at East London carrying him past Jimmy Hunter's record of 49 tries for New Zealand. Less satisfying was the goalkicking. Usually a part-timer in such matters, Williams found himself thrust into the role of kicker . . . and didn't like it. When he placed a goal against Eastern Province it was the All Blacks' first place-kick success from 16 attempts on tour.

With shortcomings at fullback and in goalkicking, and in difficulties in the scrums after Brad Johnstone and Kerry Tanner were incapacitated, the All Blacks slumped to a 3–1 series defeat, the Springboks unquestionably being assisted by operating under their own referees.

Beegee confesses that he and Ian Kirkpatrick had tears in their eyes after the fourth test, lost 15–14 after several controversial refereeing decisions. They were tears born of frustration.

THESE days Beegee assists Maurice Trapp in coaching the fabulously successful Auckland team which has been undefeated in national championship play since 1986.

Twelve months later Beegee had the satisfaction of being on the winning side when the series — against Phil Bennett's British Lions — was decided, also by one point, in the fourth test at Eden Park.

But luck was to desert the great winger totally three months later, in the first test against France in Toulouse. Having scored an important try during the first spell, Williams had hopes of making it a double when Bruce Robertson lobbed him a pass, with the overlap, late in the game. Beegee lunged for the ball and secured it, but after an ankle-tap from Guy Noves he began to stumble. Virtually out of control, he felt muscles tear inside his leg, and an instant later he was crash-tackled by fullback Michel Aguirre.

The damage was horrifying. The thigh bone of the left leg was dislocated, and all the hip muscles torn. It meant several days, totally incapacitated, in hospital in Toulouse before arrangements were made to fly him back to New Zealand. He made the trip in unglamorous style on a stretcher.

Many expected that injury to bring an abrupt finish to Williams' career, but he battled back bravely, to play in the tests against the 1978 Wallabies and then participate in the triumphant Grand Slam tour of Britain, getting a try in what was his final All Black appearance — against the Barbarians in Cardiff.

Mighty Beegee continued his rugby for Auckland in 1979 and for Ponsonby in 1980 and 1981, being named, by a panel of sports writers in 1980, the New Zealand rugby player of the decade.

John Hart used him most effectively at fullback when he took over the Auckland team in 1982 in what represented the commencement of Auckland's golden era.

Beegee retired after that but wasn't too long out of the limelight.

In 1987, Maurice Trapp was appointed coach of Auckland and took on board Williams as his assistant.

After four years they can reflect on stunning success, being unbeaten in national championship games and still holders of the Ranfurly Shield after 40 defences. ■

Beegee – the wonder winger is reproduced from *Rugby Greats*, written by Bob Howitt and first published in 1975 by Moa Publications.

THE MAGIC OF THE RANFURLY SHIELD

By LINDSAY KNIGHT

HAPPINESS is winning the Ranfurly Shield. Youthful looking superstars Joe Stanley and John Kirwan pose with No 8 Glenn Rich and the prized trophy after Auckland's epic 28–23 win over Canterbury at Lancaster Park

Photo by : PETER BUSH

The Ranfurly Shield is New Zealand sport's most famous trophy. It is the nearest many provincial rugby players come to appearing in a test match and has provided many New Zealanders with a host of memories as they have become involved in shield rugby's triumphs and disappointments.

Many matches have been won in the last minute ... in 1960 when Waka Nathan scored a famous try for Auckland or in 1954 when Derek Mayo scored one for Canterbury.

The shield, or the "Log of Wood" as it has been nicknamed, has been played for since 1904. It was presented to the New Zealand Rugby Union in 1902 by the then Governor, the Earl of Ranfurly, for provincial competition.

It was made in England from oak timber and the silversmith, being English, when told the engraving on its face had to typify football naturally thought of soccer. So the players that have been engraved on the front are actually engaged in a game of soccer.

That, however, has not stopped the shield becoming a term synonymous with New Zealand rugby.

The first holder of the shield was Auckland, with the New Zealand union giving it the award because it had the best results of any provincial side in 1903. But from then on the shield has been decided on a challenge basis and the first match was played in 1904 between Auckland and Wellington, with Wellington winning 6-3.

At the end of the 1905 season Auckland regained the shield and then, until 1913, made 23 consecutive defences, the first of the great shield eras.

There was, however, little of the "fever" which would become associated with shield matches in later years.

In fact, in those years holding the shield was regarded as something of a nuisance and because of the costs involved few unions were prepared to make challenges. In 1909 the lack of interest meant only one shield match was played in the entire season.

When Wellington had the shield just after the end of World War One, it placed so little value on it that it was put at stake in every match it played, whether at home or away. In 1920 Wellington played an astonishing 11 shield games before losing to Southland.

Through the 1920s Southland and Hawkes Bay followed Wellington's example by putting the shield at stake in occasional away games.

But the practice petered out as holding unions began to guard the shield with ever more jealousy and it was not till 1988 that there was a return to away shield games.

The present great Auckland side has put the shield at stake in the past three years in matches in Te Kuiti, New Plymouth, Napier, Paeroa, Ashburton and Gisborne.

The shield first became the prize above all others in provincial rugby when Hawkes Bay became the holder in 1922 and held it for 24 consecutive games until 1927.

The Hawkes Bay side was called "The Magpies" because of its black and white jerseys.

Its coach was Norman McKenzie and he went out to remote country areas and found players who would become some of the best New Zealand has had, men like fullback George Nepia and the Brownlie brothers, Maurice and Cyril.

THE immensity of the crowd is apparent here as Terry Wright scores one of the tries which ended Canterbury's three year tenure of the shield in 1985.

Photo by : PETER BUSH

THE shield has incurred more than its share of controversy down the years, most recently in the final challenge of the 1990 season when Canterbury refused to play scrums after its hooker was sent off. In action from that eventful encounter, flanker Rob Penney fires out a pass watched by team mates, from left, Graeme Bachop, Phil Cropper, Dallas Seymour, Richard Ewins and Ian Fleming.   Photo by : KENJI ITO

At its peak the Hawkes Bay seemed to be as unbeatable as the Auckland side is today.

In 1926 it beat Wairarapa 77–14, Wanganui 36–3, Wellington 58–8, Auckland 41–11 and Canterbury at Lancaster Park in Christchurch 17–15 when it gave away the home ground advantage.

When Hawkes Bay eventually lost the shield it caused an argument in New Zealand rugby greater even than that when in 1990 scrums were suspended in the match between Auckland and Canterbury.

Wairarapa early in 1927 caused an upset by beating Hawkes Bay. In the return just over a month later, though, Hawkes Bay won and recaptured the shield.

Or so everyone thought. But because Hawkes Bay had played a man named Wattie Barclay Wairarapa protested that he was not residentially qualified to play.

The New Zealand union upheld the protest and so Hawkes Bay lost by being disqualified.

It caused a sensation at the time and through the years shield rugby has been studded with similar controversies.

Some unions have declined challenges from others when it has not suited them to play. In 1978, for example, just after beating Manawatu, North Auckland refused to play Otago and Southland. In 1974 there was an argument, too, when Marlborough and Poverty Bay couldn't agree over which jerseys they should wear. Both have a similar plain red jersey.

The shield used to cause so many arguments that once a mayor of a town sent a telegram to his local side urging them to win the shield but when they were coming home on the inter-island ferry to throw it into Cook Strait. The team replied it would do this only if the shield was tied round the mayor's neck.

As the argument over Canterbury not wanting scrums against Auckland showed, people can still get stirred up when the interests of their home sides are affected. But in recent years there has not been quite the same number of disagreements because the New Zealand union has tightened the rules.

Some of the disputes have been caused by the challenge system, which meant a holder was limited to seven or eight matches a year. Thus teams have been known to go several seasons without a chance of a challenge and when a union had a good side that seemed unfair. However, the tighter rules and the introduction of the national championship in 1976, plus the gesture of unions like Auckland taking the shield on tour, appears to have removed some of the unfairness.

As well as Hawkes Bay in the 1920s, other great eras have been by Otago (20 successful defences in the 1940s when the coach was Vic Cavanagh junior), Waikato in the early 1950s when their mascot became known as "Mooloo", Canterbury in the mid-1950s, Auckland in the early 1960s and Hawkes Bay in the late 1960s. Generally it's the big unions who hold the shield but in 1973 little Marlborough had some glory by causing a huge upset against Canterbury.

But the most successful Ranfurly Shield side has been the present Auckland champions. It took the shield in a famous game against another fine side in Canterbury. When Alex Wyllie had been its coach Canterbury defended the shield 25 consecutive times between 1982 and 1985. That meant it equalled the record Auckland had put up between 1960 and 1963 when the coach had been Fred Allen.

Since beating Canterbury 28–23 in 1985 Auckland has now defended the shield on 40 consecutive occasions. Many are now saying it can extend the record to 50.

Auckland's long reign means it has gathered in a host of other records. Terry Wright and Zinzan Brooke now have scored 37 tries each in Ranfurly Shield matches. That means they are now seven ahead of a Hawkes Bay winger of the 1920s, Bert Grenside.

Many thought at the time his record might never be beaten. And Auckland's remarkable goalkicker Grant Fox now has 665 points in shield rugby. That's nearly twice as many as the previous record holder, Robbie Deans, who in turn had scored more than twice as many as the next man, Ian Bishop.

And when Auckland beat Thames Valley 97–0 in 1986 that was the biggest score in a shield match. But it should be remembered that for many years the value of a try was only three points.

When it beat Wairarapa 77–14 in 1926 Hawkes Bay scored 17 tries so if that game was played today the score would have been 94–16.

Only one other side has scored 17 tries in a shield game: Canterbury when it beat North Otago 88–0 in 1983. ■

TWO of the stars of the record-breaking Auckland team in 1990 — winger Va'aiga Tuigamala and second-five Bernie McCahill.

Photo by : KENJI ITO

Lindsay Knight is the rugby correspondent for the *Dominion Sunday Times,* having previously held that position with the *Auckland Star.* He is the author of *Kirky* and *Shield Fever,* successful rugby publications.

FASCINATION IS RUMMAGING THROUGH A RUGBY MUSEUM

By HEATHER KIDD

JUST a few of the hundreds of fascinating exhibits on display at the Rugby Museum in Auckland.

Photo by : KENJI ITO

IF YOU'RE into rugby literature, the Rugby Museum is a treasure trove. More than 1000 books and countless programmes reflect the great matches and great events over the decades.
Photo by : KENJI ITO

Royalty seldom offers autographs to the general public which is why, at the Rugby Museum in Auckland's Fort Street, a yellowing luncheon menu has such pride of place.

For there in one corner is scrawled Edward P just underneath the signature of one of New Zealand's Invincibles, Cyril Brownlie.

The farewell luncheon was in honour of the All Blacks of 1924–25, the men who played and won 28 matches in Great Britain, including tests against Ireland, Wales and England followed by two games in France and two more victories.

Altogether the team scored 721 points while conceding just 112.

The luncheon was hosted by the Sportsmen of the Motherland and took place in the Piccadilly Hotel on January 21, 1925.

Guests dined on Les Hors d'oeuvre a la Porter, Le Consomme Richardson en tasse, La Timbale de sole a la Nicolls, Le Poulet de printemps Wakefield, Les Haricots verts nouveaux de Nepia, la Salade Cooke and La Vasque de poires Brownlie.

Wines, a Chateau La Flora Blanche Etampe and Chateau Pontet Canet 1917, helped wash down the fine fare and patrons finished the banquet with coffee, a Dean Special.

Guests at the luncheon were a who's who, both of the rugby world and English aristocracy.

The head table included Lord Desborough, the vice-president of the British Olympic Association, New Zealand's High Commissioner, the Hon Sir James Allen KCB, General Sir Ian Hamilton GCB, GCMG, KCB and DSO, General Sir William Birdwood GCB, KCMG and commander of the Australian and New Zealand Corps in France, General Sir Alexander Godley KCB and KCMG, the Earl Cadogan CBE and chairman of the British Olympic Association, Lord Ashfield, the Earl of Lonsdale and other titled gentlemen.

The most notable guest was, of course, the Prince of Wales, Prince Edward and he sat at the top table alongside these

PROBABLY the most prized possessions at the Rugby Museum are Cyril Brownlie's collection of souvenirs from the famous 1924–25 Invincibles tour. Brownlie won notoriety by being ordered off against England at Twickenham — an incident vividly captured on camera.

Photo by : KENJI ITO

peers of the realm and two of the All Black team, Cliff Porter the captain and Stan Dean the manager.

Down on table D, along with George Nepia, Les Cupples and several other All Blacks, sat Cyril Brownlie.

Two-and-a-half weeks prior to the luncheon Brownlie had been the recipient of a dubious honour when he was ordered from the field early in the England international at Twickenham, thus becoming the first All Black to be sent off, an event that has occurred just one time since when Colin Meads received his marching orders during the 1964 test against Scotland at Murrayfield.

The story goes that once showered and dressed Brownlie was invited to watch the remainder of the match with the Prince of Wales.

Perhaps the two men struck up a friendship that resulted in the prince putting his autograph on Brownlie's menu.

The menu is just one of the fascinating items of Brownlie memorabilia contained in a special glass case.

There's the travelling trunk, rather battered and worn, the same one as used in the Steinlager commercials where the young boy lifts out the old All Black jersey, pulls it on and becomes a man.

Clothes do not always maketh the man but many a diet must have needed to be carefully watched during the long tour so that the Kiwi travellers did not burst out of their gear.

Travel was by ship which meant weeks at sea, being faced with such temptations as the breakfast menu offering a selection of fruits, cereals, fish, six egg dishes, ham or bacon, steak and onions and chips, veal cutlets, roast chicken and griddle cakes and maple syrup.

Lunch was little different. How would you choose between fresh scallops or Pondicherry curry and rice? Or what about Parisian steak or York ham. Then there's always jam roll pudding or peach pie to finish off.

It's not like that in the 1990s.

Other items of interest from Brownlie's collection include his blazers and a whistle which is said to be the one referee

Albert Freethy used in the All Blacks' test against England.

The battered trunk contains many letters and old photographs. There's a note from Bill Hazlett inviting "Tonk" to his wedding and letters of congratulations and adoration from Brownlie's many fans.

There is a delightful photograph taken during a team picnic, men dressed in full suits, waistcoats and hats, perched on rocks and eating off plates with knives and forks.

Cyril Brownlie was from a renowned Hawkes Bay rugby family. His brother Maurice, a man many said was the more accomplished footballer, was also a member of the Invincibles.

Cyril, a farmer, collapsed and died while working on a fence line in 1954 aged 57.

Memorable moments in New Zealand rugby history are carefully documented and well displayed at the Rugby Museum. There's a Ranfurly Shield corner with a large portrait of Lord Ranfurly, the donor of the famous log o' wood, hold-

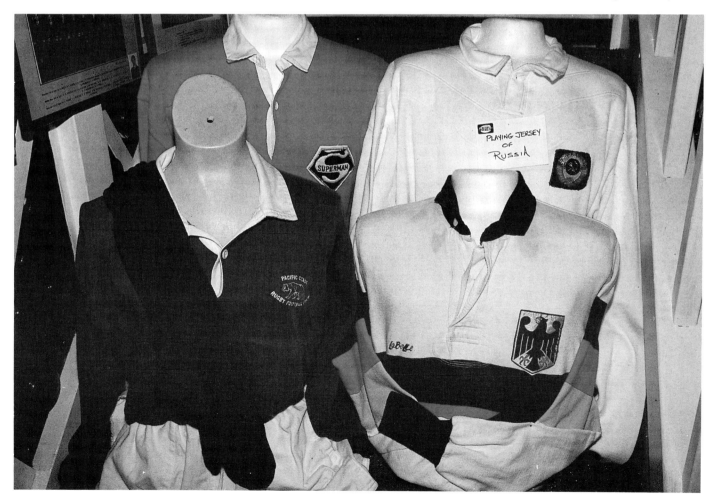

HOW many of these rugby jerseys are you familiar with? The Superman club is of Japan, the Russian jersey has been sighted in Australia but not yet in New Zealand, the eagle represents West Germany and the maroon jersey of the Pacific Coast of America is a souvenir from the first women's rugby test against New Zealand at Christchurch in 1988.

Photo by : KENJI ITO

ing pride of place. Ranfurly presented the Shield to New Zealand in 1902 and its long and exciting history fills a wall.

Heroes, prominent coaches and captains of distinction feature in charts that have recorded the eras of the great Ranfurly Shield sides — Hawkes Bay, North Auckland, Canterbury, Waikato, Wellington and Auckland.

The corner, and indeed most of the museum, is crammed with books. Of special interest are two treasured copies of the bible of New Zealand rugby *Men In Black*. You can find every *Almanack*, bar a couple of the earliest editions, and a full set of the *Rugby Annuals*.

There are over 1000 books, a selection of delights for rugby buffs — biographies, autobiographies, tour analyses (many by the doyen of New Zealand rugby writers, TP McLean), fitness hints, rugby for beginners, rugby for the purist, rugby for the fans ... it's all there. Has any game ever encouraged more eloquent, more passionate prose?

Programmes also feature prominently in this hall of rugby fame. The older ones, New Zealand versus England at Twickenham in 1954 and the British Isles versus New Zealand in 1950, are pinned to the wall alongside those from more modern times.

Old programmes cost a shilling and then, in the early days of decimal currency, 20 cents, a far cry from the four or five dollars of today's test programmes.

No one, no part of New Zealand's national game, has been forgotten. There is a delightful photo display from the Auckland club final of 1968. Manukau defeated Ponsonby 20–16 in front of a crowd of 18,000 at Eden Park.

An even more spectacular photo features the final 1937 test at Eden Park between the All Blacks and the Springboks. The South Africans won 17–6 in front of a massive crowd. It looks as if all New Zealand turned up to watch the match, a graphic reminder of how important rugby has been to this country.

Another group of photographs contains baby pictures of the 1972 All Blacks. Can you spot Joe Karam, Keith Murdoch and George Skudder? Is that really Grant Batty, that chubby romper-suited baby with a full head of curly hair? And what about Bryan Williams dressed in a jumper and nothing else to display a lot more than a wide smile!

Auckland referee Glenn Wahlstrom features as a life-size cardboard cutout and All Black selectors, past and present, Earle Kirton and Alex Wyllie are painted on a passage wall. Kirton's signature, his cap, scarf and cigar make him easily recognisable. Wyllie looks younger, less worried than he often has in 1990.

One of the more recent introductions to the game, a sideline highlight, cheerleaders, have earned a piece of wall. There are plenty of photos showing Hollywood-type smiles and lots of long legs.

Jerseys from all over the world hang high. Have you ever heard of the Tonyrefail Rugby Club, the team from Tumble or Nantyglo? Jerseys from famous university sides Oxford and Cambridge are there, as are the official jerseys from Russia, Yugoslavia, Sweden and Germany.

Andy Haden's Cavaliers' jersey is there, as is his first All Black one, worn so proudly back in 1972.

The training gear Grant Fox wore during the 1987 World Cup campaign, plus boots, are enclosed in a glass cabinet.

And who said using rugby players to advertise products is a modern phenomenon?

Back in 1926 the New Zealand Maoris team to France and England was used to endorse, of all products, flour.

The team photo appeared with a newspaper advertisement that read: "ThoroughBreds — all reared on Champion muscle raiser flour, December 1926. The famous New Zealand All Black Maori football team which has met with such success during its tour of France and England. Northern Roller Milling Co Ltd, Auckland."

Rugby balls, rugby caps (some dating back to last century) are on display. Ties and socks, tankards and plaques — they're all there, each one, every item a piece of New Zealand's glorious rugby history.   ∎

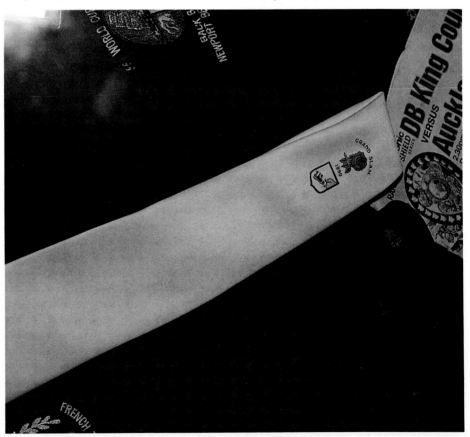

AND here's something different — England's 1990 Grand Slam tie. The only problem is ... England didn't win the Grand Slam this year. Scotland did. The tie maker who anticipated an English victory reran them all with a boot being delivered to a rear end (presumably an English player's!).

Photo by : KENJI ITO

Heather Kidd as the assistant editor of *Rugby News* became the first woman to be attached to major international touring teams. A novelist and successful journalist she was named New Zealand sports writer of the year for 1990. She currently lives in Limerick, Ireland, where her husband is rugby coaching.

RUGBY BOOKS – THE MAN WHO HAS THEM ALL

If there's anything you want to know about rugby literature, contact Dave McLaren in Dunedin. He's surely the nation's leading gatherer of books on the game, claiming to have virtually every significant rugby work published with a couple of minor (and extremely rare) exceptions.

Because of his passion for such books, in 1985 he published a bibliography called *A Handbook of Rugby Literature* which has proved invaluable for book-collecting buffs of which there are many hundreds throughout New Zealand.

Since 1985 Dave McLaren reports that there have been more than 200 new entries and so in 1990 he has published the second edition of his handbook.

It details every New Zealand book on the sport ever published and all the important overseas ones.

He concludes his valuable work with some fascinating tables.

He lists the 10 rarest books on rugby in New Zealand, the 10 rugby books every library should have, what he regards as the 10 best and 10 worst books on the game and the most prolific authors.

If you'd like to subscribe to Dave McLaren's *Handbook of Rugby Literature*, write to him at 219 High Street, Dunedin. The book sells for $NZ25.00 (including postage).

Here are his lists:

THE 10 RAREST BOOKS ON RUGBY IN NEW ZEALAND

1. *The New Zealand Tour 1901* – JR Henderson. (One copy known in New Zealand.)
2. *The Northern Tour of the Dunedin Football Club 1877* – SE Sleigh. (Two copies known in New Zealand.)
3. *Rugby Football – Some Present Day New Zealand Methods* – EAP Cockroft (1924). (Two copies known in New Zealand.)
4. *On The Ball* – B Giles (1935).
5. *The New Zealand Rugby Football Annual 1885* – SE Sleigh.
6. *With the British Rugby Team in Maoriland* – RA Barr (1908).
7. *The Art of Rugby Football* – TR Ellison (1902).
8. *Rugby Football Past and Present – The Tour of the Native Team* – T Eyton (1896).
9. *The Complete Rugby Footballer* – D Gallaher and WJ Stead (1906).
10. *The Triumphant Tour of the New Zealand Footballers* – GH Dixon (1906).

The lower the number, the rarer the book.

THE 10 RUGBY BOOKS THAT ALL NEW ZEALAND RUGBY LIBRARIES SHOULD HAVE

1. *The Encyclopaedia of New Zealand Rugby* – RH Chester & NAC McMillan.
2. *Centenary – 100 Years of All Black Rugby* – RH Chester & NAC McMillan.
3. *Great Days in New Zealand Rugby* – TP McLean.
4. *Fifteen Men on a Dead Man's Chest* – M Ball.
5. *Shield Fever* – L Knight.
6. *The World of Rugby* – W Reyburn.
7. *Springbok Saga* – C Greyvenstein.
8. *Australian Rugby Union* – J Pollard.
9. *On The Ball* – G Slatter.
10. *New Zealand Rugby Skills and Tactics* – I Vodanovich (Ed.).

THE 10 BEST BOOKS ON RUGBY

1. *Great Days in New Zealand Rugby* – TP McLean.
2. *The Complete Rugby Footballer* – D Gallaher and W Stead.
3. *Rugby Football Past and Present – The Tour of the Native Team* – T Eyton.
4. *The Great Fight of the French Fifteen* – D Lalanne.
5. *Fifteen Men on a Dead Man's Chest* – M Ball.
6. *The Bennie Osler Story* – C Greyvenstein.
7. *The Rugby Companion* – W Reyburn.
8. *Rugby Football Internationals Roll of Honour* – EHD Sewell.
9. *Pathway Among Men* – JT Burrows.
10. *New Zealand Rugby Legends* – TP McLean.

THE 10 WORST BOOKS ON RUGBY

1. *The Complete Who's Who of International Rugby* – Godwin.
2. *Rugby Handbook* – Craven.
3. *Total Rugby – Think Rugby* – both by Greenwood. (I'm cheating here.)
4. *Great Moments in Sport – Rugby Football* – Thomas.
5. *For the Record* – Gault.
6. *The Lighter Side of All Black Rugby* – Anonymous.
7. *The Mighty Lions* – Reason.
8. *Tries* – Davies.
9. *The Science of Rugby Football* – Davis & Ireland.
10. *Rugby Is A Funny Game* – Brown, Ripley et al.

And there are many, many more!

PROFILE : PHILIPPE SELLA

Full name: Philippe Jean-Paul Sella.
Birthdate: February 14, 1962.
Zodiac sign: Aquarius.
Birthplace: Clairac.
Residence: Agen.
Occupation: Sales promoter.
Height: 1.81m.
Weight: 84kg.
Marital status: Married.
Children: A daughter (Philippine).
Years playing rugby: Started playing when I was 10-years-old (1972).
Position: Centre-threequarter since 1981. Before then played variously at fullback and flyhalf.
Present club: Agen.
Previous club: Clairac.
International experience: Has played 63 tests for France (the most capped centre). First cap against Romania in 1982.
Most difficult opponents: Danie Gerber and John Kirwan.
Best rugby memory: The World Cup semi-final against Australia in Sydney.
Biggest disappointment: Missing out on the Grand Slam in 1984 when we lost to Scotland.
Favourite countries: Mauritius in the Indian Ocean; New Zealand.
Biggest influence on career: Having a coach who taught me to respect others and to enjoy sport regardless of the result.
Other sports/leisure interests: Water skiing, golf; my main leisure interest is spending time with my wife and daughter.
Favourite rugby ground: Le Parc des Princes, Paris.
Favourite films: *Midnight Express* made a big impact on me. Otherwise *Les Miserables*.
Favourite TV shows: *Ushuaia*. (A French programme; a cross between sport and adventure.)
Favourite music: French singers Francis Gabrel and Jean-Jacques Goldman; Dire Straits.
Favourite food: Salmon with sorrel sauce or fresh foie gras served hot.
Funniest rugby experience: Listening to Patrick Esteve tell a series of jokes after a match in 1982.

PROFILE : SERGE BLANCO

Full name: Serge Albert Blanco.
Birthdate: August 31, 1958.
Zodiac sign: Virgo.
Birthplace: Caracas, Venezuela.
Residence: Biarritz, France.
Occupation: Public relations.
Height: 1.84m.
Weight: 85kg.
Marital status: Married to Liliane.
Children: Sebastien and Stephan.
Years playing rugby: Started playing in 1973 (15-years-old).
Position: Fullback. Has played 10 or 11 games for France on the wing (1981–82).
Present club: Biarritz Olympique.
International experience: 76 caps (most capped French player). First played for France versus South Africa, 1980. Record tryscorer for France in tests.
Most difficult opponents: All Blacks and Springboks.
Best rugby memory: My next match.
Most memorable match: My next match.
Biggest disappointment: Never being champion of France with my club Biarritz. For me the World Cup in 1987 was not a disappointment — it's a wonderful memory.
Favourite countries: New Zealand for rugby; Argentina on the personal or human level; Hawaii for tourism.
Biggest influence on career: Michel Celaya without a doubt.
Other sports/leisure interests: Anything and everything; tennis, skiing, football, "pleto basque"; my family.
Favourite rugby ground: Le Parc des Princes, Paris.
Favourite films: All good films, especially those with a message or deal with human relations, like *One Flew Over the Cuckoo's Nest, Midnight Express*. Have a soft spot for humorous French films like *Les Ripoux, La Grande Vadrouille* or any film with Louis de Funes.
Favourite TV shows: *Mediations*. (A French programme where experts debate on current problems — education, pollution, crime etc.)
Favourite music: Jean-Michel Jarre.
Favourite food: French cuisine of course. No particular dishes, just everything that is good. I am a "grand gourmand" and a "grand gourmet".
Biggest drag in rugby: People who cheat, at whatever level.

RUGBY HUMOUR – FRENCH STYLE

That rugby transcends language barriers is delightfully illustrated in this selection of cartoons by Frenchman Pat Mallet. They are reproduced from his book *Les Mordus du Rugby*, published in Paris by le cherche midi editeur.

PROFILE : TIM HORAN

Full name: Timothy James Horan.
Birthdate: May 18, 1970.
Zodiac sign: Taurus.
Birthplace: Sydney.
Residence: Brisbane.
Occupation: Sales representative.
Height: 1.82m.
Weight: 84kg.
Marital status: Single.
Position: Centre, second-five.
Present club: Souths, Brisbane.
Most difficult opponent: Joe Stanley.
Best rugby memories: Third test versus New Zealand, 1990; first test versus France, 1989.
Biggest disappointment: Injury to knee versus France, first test, 1990.
Favourite country: Australia.
Biggest influence on career: John Elders, coach of first XV, Downlands College, Toowoomba.
Other sports/leisure interests: Horse-racing, golf, going to the coast.
Favourite rugby ground: Ballymore.
Favourite film: *Major league.*
Favourite TV show: *Wide World of Sports.*
Favourite music: Jimmy Barnes.
Favourite food: T-bone steak and chips.
Funniest rugby experience: Knowing Jason Little.
Biggest drag in rugby: After-match functions.

PROFILE : DAVID CAMPESE

Full name: David Campese.
Birthdate: October 21, 1962.
Zodiac sign: Libra.
Birthplace: Queanbeyan.
Residence: Sydney or Italy.
Occupation: Public relations officer.
Height: 1.78m.
Weight: 83kg.
Marital status: Single.
Years playing rugby: 11.
Position: Fullback or wing.
Present club: Randwick.
International experience: 53 caps, against New Zealand, British Lions, four Home Unions, Fiji, France, Argentina, USA, Japan and Italy.
Most difficult opponent: Everybody.
Best rugby memory: Barbarians match 1988.
Most memorable match: All the games I have lost.
Biggest disappointment: Losing.
Favourite countries: Ireland, Italy and Scotland.
Biggest influence on career: Bob Dwyer and Mark Ella.
Other sports/leisure interests: Tennis, golf, swimming.
Favourite rugby grounds: Sydney Cricket Ground and Athletic Park (where I've won three tests out of three).
Favourite films: *Indiana Jones 1, 2* and *3.*
Favourite TV show: *Batman.*
Favourite music: Everything.
Favourite food: Pasta.
Funniest rugby experience: Dropping the ball 25 metres out in 1988 Barbarians match.
Biggest drag in rugby: Training and living out of a suitcase.

THE OTHER OPTION
REFEREEING

By BRIDGET GEE

As you consider the options for your future in the game of rugby, take a look at the referee and ask yourself if you would have the dedication and strength for this job.

Being a referee differs from being a player in that you are the one and only person with a whistle on the field! As a player, you have 14 mates out there with you, giving you support and you supporting them. The ref is alone to control 30 players who all want to have a good game of rugby. Much is expected of the referee — could you measure up to the task? What is expected of a referee in today's fast moving game of rugby?

Firstly, the referee — man or woman — must *want* to be a referee. And like any player, you must be fit enough to keep up with the play. But fitness is not only physical. You must be mentally fit to be able to instantly judge a situation and react. Concentration for the full 80 minutes is the key.

Realise you are alone out on the field and that your responsibility is to those two teams. They want consistency from you. You must know your law — no matter how unusual the incident — so that you can apply these fairly to both teams. Understand that each game is played under different conditions by different teams of differing skills and maturity. By this I mean the referee must understand the intention of the law as well as the wording.

The referee is like the team captain or coach — he or she is in a position of authority and must gain the respect of the players and be able to "manage" them. A good referee strikes a rapport with the players, communicating by voice and whistle to control the game. You must also have a tough skin! Because although you are dedicated to your task, there are sometimes those on the sideline who don't see eye-to-eye with your decisions! To a good referee, comments from the (often one-eyed) crowd are background noise only.

You can be as ambitious as a referee as you can a player. There are opportunities in refereeing to advance to international level but everyone has to start from the bottom!

As a first year referee, you are likely to be appointed to games ranging from under-11 to under-13 age groups. This is a great level to start at and learn the ropes. You will get a lot of help from senior referees in your association. Weekly "classes" are held where you talk about games and problems or incidents that occurred and you learn. Not just about the law but about the game.

From this level you can progress up through the ranks to as far as you want or you are able. Every Referees' Association in New Zealand has a "coaching and grading" panel who come and watch your game and grade you for promotion. This is a helpful way to find out your strengths and weaknesses and make adjustments for both.

There are two written examinations which you can sit. These are set by the New Zealand Rugby Referees' Association and are the official qualification required to advance to the most senior levels of refereeing. Because refereeing requires accuracy, the mark to pass each exam is 80 per cent.

If you have the dedication and skill to become a top referee in your Association, you may then be selected to officiate provincial matches. What a thrill to run out on to Eden Park to referee Auckland

NEW ZEALAND'S top-ranking referee, David Bishop, in action at Twickenham.

Photo by : MIKE BRETT, UK

AUSTRALIA'S top referee Kerry Fitzgerald translates for French captain Daniel Dubroca during the World Cup in 1987.

Photo by : PETER BUSH

and Otago! From there, the two very best referees in the country are picked for the international panel. You could be appointed to control the France versus England Five Nations match! If you have the commitment, skill and dedication, this could be *you*!

There are a lot of people who take up refereeing after finishing their playing careers. Australia's No 1 referee, Kerry Fitzgerald, was a representative player in Queensland. Former All Black Grahame Thorne gets out on to the field every weekend in winter — but not to play. He, like many "retired" players, wants to put something back into the game that gave him so much, so he referees.

But *you* don't need to wait until your playing career is over. Consider refereeing as an option. The younger you start, the more chance you will have of making it to international level at a young age. You'll be just as fit, you will know more about rugby and the "man management" skills you will acquire will help you in your life "off the field".

If you want to find out more about becoming a referee in the future, contact your local rugby club or rugby union office for information.

Bridget Gee is a rugby referee in the Auckland Rugby Referees' Association.
She is in her fourth year as an active referee and controls matches up to under-21 and senior restricted level.
She is 26 and manages a publishing company.

The New Zealand Rugby Union has a Fair Play Code designed to ensure the enjoyment and satisfaction of young participants in the game of rugby.

Contrary to popular belief, children should play rugby to satisfy themselves, not necessarily adults or members of their own peer group.

The Fair Play Code hopes to encourage youth participation in rugby by making it attractive, safe and enjoyable for children.

INTRODUCTION

The code is designed:

• to return the elements of enjoyment and satisfaction to the child participant;

• to make adults aware that children play to satisfy themselves and not necessarily to satisfy adults or members of their own peer group;

• to improve the physical fitness of young by encouraging participation in rugby by making it attractive, safe and enjoyable for all children.

COACH'S CODE

1. Be reasonable in your demands on the young players' time, energy and enthusiasm. Remember that they have other interests.

2. Teach your players that rules of the game are mutual agreements which no one should evade or break.

3. Group players according to age, height, skill and physical maturity whenever possible.

4. Avoid over-playing the talented players. The "just average" players need and deserve equal time.

5. Remember that children play for fun and enjoyment and that winning is only part of it. Never ridicule or yell at the children for making mistakes or losing a game.

6. Ensure that equipment and facilities are appropriate to the age and ability of the players.

7. The scheduling and length of practice times and games should take into consideration the maturity level of the children.

8. Develop team respect for the ability of opponents, as well as for the judgement of referees and opposing coaches.

9. Follow the advice of a doctor in determining when an injured player is ready to play again.

10. Remember that children need a coach they can respect. Be generous with your praise when it is deserved and set a good example.

11. Make a personal commitment to keep yourself informed on sound coaching principles and the principles of growth and development of children.

PARENT'S CODE

1. Do not force an unwilling child to participate in rugby.

2. Remember, children are involved in rugby for their enjoyment, not yours.

3. Encourage your child always to play by the rules.

4. Teach your child that honest effort is as important as victory so that the result of each game is accepted without undue disappointment.

5. Turn defeat into victory by helping your child work towards skill improvement and good sportsmanship. Never ridicule or yell at your child for making a mistake or losing a game.

6. Remember that children learn best by example. Applaud good play by your team and by members of the opposing team.

7. Do not publicly question the referee's judgement and never his/her honesty.

8. Support all efforts to remove verbal and physical abuse from children's rugby.

9. Recognise the value and importance of volunteer coaches. They give of their time and resources to provide recreational activities for your child.

TEACHER'S CODE

1. Encourage children to develop basic skills and avoid over-specialisation in positional play during their formative years.

2. Create opportunities to teach sportsmanship, just as you would in teaching the basic skills.

3. Ensure that efforts for both skill improvement and good sportsmanship are rewarded by praise.

4. Remember that players are also students so be reasonable in your demands on their energy and enthusiasm.

5. Ensure that skill learning and free play activities have priority over highly structured competitions for very young children.

6. Prepare children for inter-class and inter-school competitions by first providing instruction in the skills required.

7. Make a personal commitment to keep yourself informed on sound coaching principles and the principles of growth and development of children.

8. Help children understand the fundamental philosophical differences between the games they play and adult games shown on television.

9. Help children understand the responsibilities and implications of the freedom to choose between fair and unfair play.

10. Make children aware of the physical fitness values of rugby and its lifelong recreational value.

REFEREE'S CODE

1. Modify rules and regulations to match the skill level of the players.

2. Use commonsense to ensure that the "spirit of the game" for children is not lost by "over-refereeing" the game.

3. Actions speak louder than words. Ensure that both on and off the field your behaviour is consistent with the principles of good sportsmanship.

4. Compliment both teams on their good play, whenever such praise is deserved.

5. Be consistent, objective and courteous.

6. Condemn the deliberate "good foul" as being unsportsmanlike, thus retaining respect for fair play.

7. Publicly encourage rule changes which will reinforce the principles of participation for fun and enjoyment.

8. Make a personal commitment to keep yourself informed on sound refereeing principles and the principles of growth and development of children.

ADMINISTRATOR'S CODE

1. Ensure that equal opportunities for participation in rugby are made available to all children, regardless of ability, sex, age or handicap.

2. Involve children in the planning, leadership and evaluation of the activity.

3. Do not allow the game to become primarily spectator entertainment.

4. Equipment and facilities must be appropriate to the maturity level of the children.

5. Rules and length of schedules should take into consideration the age and maturity level of the children.

6. Remember that play is done for its own sake. Play down the importance of awards.

7. Distribute a code of ethics for good sportsmanship to spectators, coaches, players, referees, parents and teachers.

8. Ensure that parents, coaches, sponsors, doctors and participants understand their authority and their responsibility for fair play in rugby.

9. Ensure that proper supervision is provided by certified or proven coaches and referees capable of promoting good

sportsmanship and good technical skills.

10. Offer clinics to improve the standards of coaching and refereeing with emphasis on good sportsmanship.

SPECTATOR'S CODE

1. Remember that children play organised sports for their own fun. They are not there to entertain you and they are not miniature All Blacks.

2. Be on your best behaviour. Don't use profane language or harass players, coaches or referees.

3. Applaud good play by your own team and the visiting team.

4. Show respect for your team's opponents. Without them there would be no games.

5. Never ridicule or scold a child for making a mistake during a game.

6. Condemn the use of violence in all forms.

7. Respect the referee's decisions.

8. Encourage players to play according to the rules.

PLAYER'S CODE

1. Play for the "fun of it", not just to please your parents or coach.

2. Play by the rules.

3. Never argue with the referee's decisions. Let your captain or coach ask any necessary questions.

4. Control your temper — no "mouthing off".

5. Work equally hard for yourself and your team — your team's performance will benefit and so will your own.

6. Be a good sport. Applaud all good play, whether by your team or by your opponents.

7. Treat all players as you yourself would like to be treated. Don't interfere with, bully or take unfair advantage of any players.

8. Remember that the goals of the game are to have fun, improve your skills and feel good. Don't be a show-off or always try to get the most points.

9. Co-operate with your coach, team mates and opponents, for without them you don't have a game. ∎

WALES' flamboyant, but extremely popular, referee Clive Norling, who has on several occasions controlled international fixtures in New Zealand.

Photo by : MIKE BRETT, UK

RUGBY SHORTS

SHE rang the fire station to report a fire.

The fireman who answered the phone said: "Look, we're in the middle of a darts game. Can you pour on some petrol and keep it going till we get there?"

■ ■ ■

ME OLD Maori mate Wi was sitting in a bar in New York passing the time away with a few beers to get rid of his jet lag when one of the locals came along and sat down beside him.

Pleasantries were exchanged and more beers consumed.

After about an hour the New York local gazing out of the window said to Wi: "See that seventy storey building out there."

"Yep," said Wi.

"Well do you know that fifty thousand people live inside it and it is that big they don't move out of it from the day they are born to the day they die."

Me old Maori mate Wi thought for a minute and turned round to the local and said: "In New Zealand we have one hundred and two thousand people living in two huts."

"Ow! Come off it Kiwi," said the local.

"Yep it's true," said Wi. "Fifty-one thousand live in the Upper Hutt and fifty-one thousand live in the Lower Hutt."

Silence!

■ ■ ■

Well, I am a Maori boy and I was born black
When I have a bath I am still black
When I am frightened I am still black
When I go out in the sun to tan, I am still black
When I am cold I am still black
And when I die, I will still be black.

Well now Pakeha, when you was born you were white
When you go and sunbathe, you go pink
When you're frightened you go more white
When you're sick you go green
When you're cold you go blue
And when you die, you go yellow.

So Pakeha, tell me who is the coloured man now?

■ ■ ■

MIKE and Paddy were out hunting and got lost in the forest. Mike said: "Now we must keep calm."

Paddy agreed: "You're right. I read that if you are lost, you should shoot three times into the air and someone will come and rescue you."

So they did this but nothing happened and they did it again and still no help came. They repeated this several times without results.

Finally Mike said: "What are we going to do now?"

And Paddy replied: "I don't know, we're almost out of arrows!"

■ ■ ■

DID YOU KNOW
... That Winston Churchill was a notable and enthusiastic spectator at the New Zealand versus France fixture in Toulouse, France in January 1925. New Zealand were led by Cliff Porter and won 30–6.
... That John Kirwan (of Auckland Marist) comes close to being our youngest All Black but has to concede to Wairarapa's Edgar Wrigley who was only 19 years and 79 days when he played for New Zealand against Australia in 1905. Pat Walsh (also of Auckland Marist then) was 19 years 106 days in 1955. Kirwan was 19 years and 184 days!
... That the first man ever to score a try for New Zealand at rugby was Harry Robert (of Wellington) who played for the 1884 All Blacks in a warm-up game against Wellington. Later on, Teddy — Harry's son — became an All Black also. Our first father and son combination!
... That the 1984 Tricolores selected 27 men for their eight game tour — whereas in 1888–89 our New Zealand Native side took away 26 men and played a colossal 107 games.

■ ■ ■

TRAVELMAN Lou Sumich was away from home when his son played the last game of the season. Lou made an expensive toll call on the Saturday night to hear the story.

His wife answered the phone and said: "Oh, Lou, it was terrible ... the poor boy broke his nose, got three stitches in his forehead, lost four front teeth and badly sprained his ankle."

Lou was impatient. "Don't waste my time and money on trivial things," he said. "I'm paying for this call ... who won?"

■ ■ ■

RON DON was at Eden Park No 2 where Grammar was playing College Rifles.

There was a bloke standing beside Ron leaning over the rail at the little cricket stand end of the ground and he kept yelling rude things at the ref and odd players.

"You're drunk!" Ron said to the man.

"Of course I am," the bloke said. "You don't think I'd come to watch Grammar sober, do you?".

Happy New Year, Ron!

■ ■ ■

AN Irishman was given the job of painting the lines in the middle of the road.

The first day he painted two miles of line, the second day one mile and the third day only about 500 yards. The boss arrived and wanted to know why he was painting less and less each day.

"Well, you see," he answered, "I keep getting foither and foither away from the paint pot."

■ ■ ■

MY NAME is not really Warren, you know. It's actually Wednesday because when I was born my parents took one look at me and said, "Let's call it a day."

■ ■ ■

DID you know that a prize was awarded to the inventor of the humble door knocker? It was called the Nobel Prize!

■ ■ ■

SOME more ways of burying the club:
1. Do nothing more than is absolutely necessary — but when other members roll up their sleeves and willingly and unselfishly use their abilities to help matters along, howl that the club is "run by a clique".
2. When a party is given, tell everybody that money is wasted on blow-outs which make a big noise and accomplish nothing.

3. When no parties are given, say the club is dead and needs a can tied to its tail.

4. Don't tell the club how it can help you but if it doesn't help — resign.

5. If you receive service without actually joining, then don't think of joining.

6. Keep your eye open for something wrong and yelp like hell when you find it.

7. Cuss the club because it acts on incomplete information.

8. Get all the club gives you but don't give it a thing.

9. Kick about the cost of membership even though it may cost no more by the week than a packet of potato crisps.

■ ■ ■

APPARENTLY when John Sims asked Linda's father for Linda's hand in marriage his future father-in-law gave him a worried look and said: "My daughter?"

"Yes sir," said polite young Johnny.

"You want to marry her."

"Yes sir."

Linda's father thought it over and then, seriously: "Have you seen my wife?

"Yes sir, I have," replied John, "but I prefer Linda."

■ ■ ■

I met him at the Hunt Club ball
In our local country hall
He was dark and handsome and very tall,
We made a date for Saturday night
And thus begun my plight
(an awesome one I won't pretend)
Of becoming a rugby player's girlfriend.

He knocked at the door
Shouted, "Did you hear the score?"
No apology for being two hours late
Considering this was our first date,
Little did I know
That there was more to come
Especially as the front row
Had lost it in the scrum,
That was the beginning of my new trend
The life of a rugby player's girlfriend.

He looked as if he'd been in a fight,
"They'd played it in the tight"
His eye was black and blue, shiny and
   closed,
His kissable lips like a tyre with the bladder exposed,
His ears a sight even sadder,
And ribs that stuck out like the rungs of
   a ladder,
He said they'd only take a few days to
   mend,
I'm a sympathetic rugby player's girl-
   friend.

The date turned out to be
Savs and pies, beer and tea,
My inaugural after-match do
Sandwiches and cakes, a story or two
Once again much to my woe
Was, what had happened in the front
   row.
The forwards lacked drive as a pack
And the backs were far too slack,
Beg your pardon,
But to understand this jargon
The next match I'll have to attend
If I'm to be a rugby player's girlfriend.

The team is made up of two packs
The forwards and the backs,
A hooker supported by two props
With short thick necks, stumpy legs,
And socks up to their hocks,
They are the front row
Packing down so low.
Inside two flankers, breakaways or Lucys
As they are sometimes named
Are the great giant locks
Dragging on the two props' jocks
And bound together by the No 8
So far I think I've got it straight.

Along the No 8 wire on the sideline
There is an almighty commotion
For someone is changing his strides
Right out in mid-ocean,
As I peep thru' my fingers
He stands crouched and lingers
He's ever so tall
And of course the strides are too small.

Next comes the halfback
He feeds the ball into the scrum
And sets the backline on their run
First-five, second-five, centre and wings,
"Out, Out, Out,"
The crowd all yell and shout,
And a long way back is the fullback
His hands have lost their touch
He's not finding the line very much,
"Tac-kill. Tac-kill. You silly buggar,"
Oh dear there's violence in this game of
   rugger.

The last man in our team is the referee
I'll meet him at the after-match spree
'Tis on him the score will depend
It's great fun being a rugby player's girl-
   friend.

For a very good reason
We were married out of season
We have two sons
Born to the smell of a wintergreen rag,
For many years they have carried the flag
They've been through the mill and are
   playing still.
As the years have evolved
Many times the boys have been told
Of Dad's exploits as a rugby fiend

And how Mum became a rugby player's
   girlfriend.
I have seen that his boots have been
   cleaned,
The gear all washed,
Sandwiches made and oranges squashed.
Now there's no more team trips
Nor the famous Peter Jones quips
No more Sunday clean-ups or elevens
And no more training from five to seven.
Coaching the thirds has gone by the way
But administration is here to stay.
This rugby story is true to life,
I know because I'm the President's wife.

ANSWERS TO TOPICAL RUGBY QUIZ

1. Homestead Rugby Stadium, **2.** Steve McDowell, **3.** Sean Fitzpatrick, **4.** 28–23, **5.** Brent Pope, **6.** Errol Brain (Counties), Gary Whetton (Auckland), Mike Brewer (Otago), Glen Fraser (Wellington), **7.** 1985, **8.** Eddie Tonks, **9.** Brian Smith, **10.** Oxford University (England), Otago University, **11.** Auckland, Waikato, Wellington, Canterbury, **12.** East Coast, **13.** Bay of Plenty, **14.** 1982, **15.** Murray Mexted, **16.** Matthew Ridge, John Schuster, Frano Botica, John Gallagher, Paul Simonsson, **17.** Marlborough, West Coast, Buller, Nelson Bays, **18.** Keith Murdoch from the 1972–73 tour of the United Kingdom and France, **19.** Jock Hobbs, **20.** (c), **21.** Andy Dalton, **22.** 1972, **23.** (b), **24.** New South Wales, **25.** Kent Lambert, **26.** Frano Botica, Bruce Deans, Andy Dalton, **27.** 19, **28.** Canterbury, Marlborough, **29.** Alan Hewson, **30.** Natal, **31.** Frank Jack (Canterbury), Glen Ross (Waikato), Russell Kemp (North Auckland), Ken Maharey (Taranaki), **32.** Softball, **33.** Kevin Schuler, **34.** Stan and John, **35.** Bryan Williams (113), Bruce Robertson (102), Colin Meads (133), Ian Kirkpatrick (113), Andy Haden (117), **36.** Don Clarke (781 points), **37.** Wilson Whineray (30 times), **38.** Stu Wilson, **39.** 74–13, **40.** Stu Wilson, **41.** John Kirwan, David Kirk, Michael Jones, **42.** Jonathon Davies, **43.** Baby Blacks, **44.** Canterbury, **45.** John Timu for John Kirwan, Kevin Schuler for Paul Henderson, **46.** Marty Berry, **47.** David Halligan, **48.** 1986, **49.** New Zealand Universities, **50.** Fred Allen, **51.** Ken and Brian Going, **52.** 1986, **53.** Bert Grenside, **54.** Thames Valley, **55.** Fiji, **56.** 1985, **57.** Canterbury, **58.** Bay of Plenty, **59.** Heather Kidd, **60.** Alex Wyllie, John Hart, Lane Penn, **61.** Viliame Ofahengaue, **62.** Ponsonby, **63.** Richard Loe, **64.** Japan (1987), **65.** Frank Oliver, **66.** Three (in 1978, 1981, 1986), **67.** Bryce Robins, **68.** Eight (by Rod Heeps against Northern New South Wales in 1962), **69.** Gary Knight (won a bronze medal for wrestling at the 1974 Christchurch Games), **70.** 1975, **71.** Dave Loveridge, **72.** True, **73.** Brian McKechnie, **74.** Chris Laidlaw, **75.** George Nepia, **76.** Stephen Pokere, **77.** The Eagles, **78.** Mark Shaw, **79.** Greg Cooper, John Timu, Arthur Stone, **80.** David Morgan (Otago), **81.** The kicking tee, **82.** Kelvin Tremain, **83.** Kawhena and Fred Woodman, **84.** Nelson Bays, **85.** Mark Donaldson, **86.** Fiji, **87.** Gary Whetton, **88.** Simon Mannix, **89.** Poverty Bay, **90.** Okara Park, **91.** John Gallagher, Craig Green, **92.** North Harbour, **93.** Ian Kirkpatrick (38), **94.** Jamie Salmon, **95.** Michael Lynagh, **96.** Hugo Porta, **97.** North Auckland, **98.** Arthur Stone, **99.** Dean Kenny, **100.** The New Zealand Maoris (12–12).

Now total up your points.
If you scored between 0 and 71 you are a *learner*.
If you scored between 72 and 92 you are an *enthusiast*.
If you scored between 93 and 121 you are a *new age expert*.
If you scored between 122 and 134 you are a *rugby freak*.

1990 ALL BLACKS TO FRANCE

BACK ROW: John Kirwan, Mike Brewer, Zinzan Brooke, Murray Pierce, Steve Gordon, Alan Whetton, Rob Gordon, Michael Jones. THIRD ROW: Walter Little, Shayne Philpott, John Timu, Joe Stanley, Bernie McCahill, Paul Henderson, Terry Wright, Kieran Crowley, Graeme Bachop. SECOND ROW: John Mayhew (doctor), Va'aiga Tuigamala, Laurence Hullena, Sean Fitzpatrick, Graham Purvis, Craig Innes, Warren Gatland, David Abercrombie (physiotherapist). FRONT ROW: Simon Mannix, John Sturgeon (manager), Steve McDowell, Gary Whetton (captain), Grant Fox, Alex Wyllie (coach), Paul McGahan.

Photo by : CANTOURIS STUDIOS